ShadowCat

Shadow**Cat**

Encountering
the American
Mountain
Lion

EDITED BY

SUSAN EWING

AND ELIZABETH

GROSSMAN

SASQUATCH BOOKS
SEATTLE

For permission to use copyrighted material, grateful acknowledgment is made to copyright holders
listed on pages 219 to 220.

Printed in the United States of America.
Distributed in Canada by Raincoast Books Ltd.
03 02 01 00 99   5 4 3 2 1

Cover photo: George Lepp/Corbis
Cover and book design: Karen Schober
Interior illustration: Sivi Ruder

Library of Congress Cataloging in Publication Data
Shadow cat : encountering the American mountain lion / edited by Susan Ewing
and Elizabeth Grossman.
          p.   cm.
     Includes bibliographical references.
     ISBN 1-57061-154-8
     1. Pumas. 2. Pumas—Political aspects—United States. I. Ewing, Susan, 1954- .
     II. Grossman, Elizabeth.
QL737.C23S49   1999
599.75'24—dc21   98-50761

Sasquatch Books
615 Second Avenue
Seattle, Washington 98104
(206) 467-4300
books@SasquatchBooks.com
http://www.SasquatchBooks.com

Sasquatch Books publishes high-quality adult nonfiction and children's books related to the
Northwest (Alaska to San Francisco). For more information about our titles, contact us at the address
above, or view our site on the World Wide Web.

Contents

Acknowledgments | *vii*

Introduction | *ix*

I. The Nature of the Beast: Natural History | *1*

SUSAN J. TWEIT   Mountain Lion | *7*

TED WILLIAMS   The Lion's Silent Return | *13*

ELIZABETH MARSHALL THOMAS   Path of the Puma | *27*

M. CATHY NOWAK   Read in Tooth and Claw | *39*

II. Tales of the Cat: Encounters | *47*

CHRIS BOLGIANO   On Not Encountering an Eastern Panther | *51*

BARBARA DEAN   A Multitude of Witnesses | *61*

TERRY TEMPEST WILLIAMS   Lion Eyes | *71*

PAM HOUSTON   Looking for Abbey's Lion | *75*

ANNICK SMITH   Wildcats I Have Not Known | *81*

JEFFERY SMITH   Plainchant for the Panther | *89*

ELLEN MELOY   Triangle | *101*

VERLYN KLINKENBORG   Riding after Lion | *107*

WARNER GLENN   San Pedro Lion | *119*

RICK BASS   Lion Story | *127*

III. Conflicts and Controversy: The Politics of Predators | *133*

JORDAN FISHER-SMITH   A Natural Death | *139*

DAVID QUAMMEN   Eat of This Flesh | *157*

E. DONNALL THOMAS, JR.   Nothing but a Hound Dog: Cats, Dogs, and Cultural Conflicts | *169*

DIANE JOSEPHY PEAVEY   The Deer with the Long Tail | *181*

HARLEY G. SHAW   Sign | *187*

WAYNE PACELLE   Bullets, Ballots, and Predatory Instincts | *199*

Notes on the Contributors | *209*

Notes on the Editors | *215*

For Further Reading | *217*

Permissions & Sources | *219*

Index | *221*

Acknowledgments

We would like to thank all of the contributors
to this collection and others—including David James Duncan,
Linda Hasselstrom, Lilly Golden, Linda Hogan, Teresa Jordan,
Bill McKibben, Richard Nelson, Brenda Peterson, and Liz Woody—
who provided encouragement and expressed enthusiasm
for the project early on. And our thanks to Gary Luke at Sasquatch
for taking on the book. Lizzie would also like to thank Cort Conley
and Jeffery Smith for their thoughts on writing about mountain lions,
as well as Sandra and Barry Lopez for their gracious hospitality,
which provided the occasion for her first sighting of a cougar.

Introduction

On a hot August day I drove over Lolo Pass, along the Lochsa
River into Idaho from Montana. In midafternoon, at the place
where the Lochsa widens as it joins the Selway and Clearwater,
I crossed the river to hike along the ridge on steep switchbacks
through shrubbery dried to an autumnal crisp of red and
orange. There were fire warnings at the trailhead. A faint haze
of smoke hung like a fine net over the cerulean sky.

    Horses had been up not long before, their leavings pungent
in the heat. I noticed some tracks among the dusty Vibram sole

and horseshoe prints. Dog or not dog, I wondered idly, looking at the neatly rounded pads. It was quiet: no scuttling of small rodents in the dry brush or twittering of birds, only a soft trickling of falling water. Far below, the river ran shallow over round rocks.

There was a quickened rustle, and no more than twenty yards ahead of me was a thick tawny tail, a set of furred shoulders, and wide ears. Cougar. It darted ahead, not turning to look at me. Instantly I retraced my steps downhill, trying not to gallop, chanting a loud nonsense mantra, hoping it would cast a spell to keep the cat from thinking me an object of prey.

At the campground I searched out the ranger, who said a cougar had been spotted in the area and that it had likely been attracted by the dead horse a team had gone up to fetch earlier that day.

It was my second cougar sighting in just over a year. The first was in July 1995 on the Pacific Crest Trail, just north of Santiam Pass above the McKenzie River in the Cascade mountains of Oregon. I had gone for a short hike. Through ponderosa, balsamroot, harebells, and penstemon I climbed, stopping to peer at the glaciers of the Three Sisters, visible to the south. It was a bright, slightly overcast day. At a clearing on the way down, I paused for a view of the peaks of Mount Washington and Three Fingered Jack. It was quiet save for insect hum. Then I heard a *thwack*, a sharp sound of movement. A large bird, I thought, and turned toward it. *A fox in a tree* was my first thought when I saw the large, furred, russet and gold creature clinging to the trunk of a tree. Then I saw the long rope of tail curled around the trunk, the wide face with light eyes and tufted ears. A big cat. What struck me first was its wide face. I'd never seen an animal in the wild with a wide face. The cat was close enough so I could see the flecks in its eyes and the cast of its nose. All four paws were around the tree. I could sense the power of its muscle and mass.

I stood utterly still, holding my breath, the words "I will not be lunch" and "Thank you" running through my head. We eyed each other for a minute or two, the big cat and I. Then it leapt off the tree and ran into a tumble of boulders on the high side of the trail. I descended swiftly, mouthing my thanks.

I have been told that people can live a lifetime in this part of the country without seeing a cougar. I have seen two in just over a year. "Perhaps the cats are trying to tell you something," said a friend. "It's a gift," said another. "Do you carry a stick?" asked yet another.

Early one spring morning in 1993, my co-editor, Susan Ewing, was leaving her house in the foothills of Bozeman, Montana, when two young cougars ran across the gravel road right in front of her truck. She said that in the gray light, it felt like magic. A few years later, from the hillside behind her house, she watched another lion through binoculars as it alternately napped and licked its paws under a big Douglas fir 500 yards from her back porch. As we talked about these experiences, we realized that although the shelves are full of books collecting stories of bears and wolves—the other iconic American predators—there was no such anthology dedicated to mountain lions. So we set out to collect contemporary accounts of this problematic and charismatic predator.

Felis concolor is a cat of many names: mountain lion, cougar, puma, panther. Elusive and reclusive, she is a shape-shifter—light and shadow, a pattern of rocks. She is a tail disappearing into dark timber, a glow of green eyeshine caught in a second of headlights. This sleek, beautiful predator is both dream and nightmare. Encounters with mountain lions are increasing as humans sprawl farther into animal territory. There have been many stories in the news of mountain lions in suburban neighborhoods and terrifying instances of cougars stalking children and hikers. As we express our concern, and wonder what this means, these powerful predators have, in many ways, become emblematic of the debate over wildness and wilderness.

Cougars once cast their shadows from the east to the west coast of North America, from Canada to South America, ranging wider than any other New World mammal. The Anasazi engraved a puma image into Arizona stone 700 years ago. Today, barely a handful of cougars hold on in the eastern United States. But protection measures instituted in recent decades in the West have allowed mountain lion populations to rebound, so the cats can still be seen from the western edge of the Great Plains to the Pacific Ocean, and from the Canadian border to Mexico.

As people and mountain lions increasingly find themselves sharing the same marginal habitat, cougar sightings are becoming more frequent. Reactions vary from a sense of privilege at this sharing of space, to fear and hostility and a culturally inherited urge to destroy the nature of wildness. Newcomers to the New World had fear but little respect for cougars, and worked systematically to remove them, trapping, shooting, and poisoning the predator into submission. Now, with little undeveloped country left on the continent, we are struggling with the definition of wilderness and the creatures that depend on it for survival: How it is to be defined? To whom does this land belong? What are our responsibilities to the land and animals?

This book presents both a consideration of these questions and a contemplation of the animal itself. It is divided into three sections: "The Nature of the Beast" looks at natural history, "Tales of the Cat" relates encounters and tells stories, and "Conflicts and Controversy" addresses issues of hunting, management, and conservation. The collection gathers stories from biologists, naturalists, guides, storytellers, conservationists, hunters, ranchers, a ranger, and residents of cougar country. Among these diverse voices and points of view, there are many common themes.

All of the writers are people whose lives bring them into contact with the wild—albeit in many different ways. Issues of wilderness and wildlife, predator and prey, and open, roadless lands inform their lives. The essays and stories raise questions about land use. Many, not so coincidentally, are stories about the destruction of habitat, which, in North America over the last 200 years, often means the cutting of forests. And all these stories are strikingly honest: there is something essential about an encounter with a mountain lion that compels one to consider one's place in the world. Among these essays the reader will also find a conversation of sorts—as writers echo one another's concerns, question others' approaches, and ponder how we deal with an animal both precious and dangerous.

—ELIZABETH GROSSMAN
Portland, Oregon
August 1998

I. The Nature of the Beast:
Natural History

In the early 1960s, after spending five years researching grizzly bears with renowned wildlife biologists Frank and John Craighead, young Maurice Hornocker was looking for a project of his own. "Tackle something tough," John encouraged the indefatigable graduate student. Rising to the challenge, Hornocker took on mountain lions.

At that time, no systematic study had been made of *Felis concolor*. The cat was considered a varmint in the western states where it still ranged, even though little was known of its numbers, its habits, or its role in the ecosystem.

Initially, Hornocker's friends and colleagues tried to dissuade him, saying it would be impossible to monitor the elusive cats. But he was determined, and willing to spend part of each winter living in a tent in the Rocky Mountain high country, where tracks in snow would offer the most illuminating reference materials.

He began his work in January 1963, marking fourteen lions within 100 miles of Missoula, Montana. By spring, hunters had killed most of his study animals. Hornocker moved the project to Idaho, eventually focusing his efforts in what is now the Frank Church–River of No Return Wilderness Area. In the wild, roadless terrain, Hornocker found his study population. . Over the next ten years, the biologist tracked collared mountain lions over thousands of miles, building a body of knowledge that became the foundation of our understanding of *Felis concolor*. Many subsequent studies have spun off Hornocker's seminal work, a number of which have been conducted by his own students under the auspices of the private, nonprofit Hornocker Wildlife Institute, founded in 1985. One of those studies crops up in the following pages. In "The Lion's Silent Return," environmental journalist Ted Williams follows researchers Ken Logan and Linda Sweanor in their study of the ecology of desert lions in New Mexico.

Before researchers advanced to questions of population dynamics, predator-prey relationships, and even predator-predator relationships, they weighed, measured, photographed, and counted, leaving us with a good basic profile of the cat. Cougar, puma, mountain lion, and panther are all names for one animal, *Felis concolor*: "cat of one color." No jaguar spots, tiger stripes, or *Felis domesticus* calico—just tawny to grayish fur with dark highlighting on the face, on the back of the ears, and at the tip of the twitching tail. Males are somewhat larger than females and size varies according to geography and prey base, so adult cats can weigh anywhere from about 75 pounds to well over 150 pounds. A large adult male can stand about two-and-a-half-feet tall at the shoulder and measure four-and-a-half-feet long from nose to hindquarter, with another three feet of tail sailing behind. A long tail enhances the lion's agility by acting as a counterweight and stabilizer for quick turns in pursuit of prey.

Mountain lions leave roundish tracks about the size of a woman's fist, with four toes and a distinctively scalloped heel pad. Like housecats, mountain lions have retractile claws, so the track doesn't show claw marks. Canine tracks are more elongated and typically leave claw impressions. When on the hunt, a lion places its hind paws in the track left by its front paws. Having already chosen the most quiet spot to step, it can then keep its eyes ahead and concentrate on stalking. This is important because the cat relies on stealth and a quick, powerful strike to knock down quarry. Felid collarbones have a shock-absorbing quality and are also designed for lateral dexterity in the front limbs. This skeletal arrangement allows cougars to wrap their front legs around trees and deer (and explains why cats are better than dogs at batting toys). On the other hand, it means that felids aren't built for running long distances at sustained high speeds. They can sprint well enough to overcome a deer out to about fifty-five yards, but they're unlikely to run down prey as would a wolf. When chased, the cougar prefers to climb a tree or hide instead of taking flight.

A mountain lion will leap onto the back of a large animal from twenty to thirty feet away and dispatch it with a crushing bite to the neck. Deer is the preferred food, but mountain lions will also hunt hares, ground squirrels, porcupines, beavers, rodents, grouse, and even elk and bighorn sheep. One big cat can eat ten pounds of meat at a single meal and needs the equivalent of one deer every seven to fourteen days to sustain itself. Domestic sheep are the most significant livestock prey, and seem to occasionally trigger a killing frenzy in which a lion kills far more animals than it can eat. Only rarely will a mountain lion eat carrion.

Native to this continent, *Felis concolor* once ranged from the

Atlantic seaboard to the Pacific coast, and from Canada deep into South America. In fact, *Felis concolor* once claimed the most extensive geographic range of any large native North American mammal. But European settlement brought an overwhelming onslaught of poisonings, bounty hunting, and habitat alteration, and today nearly all of the remaining 10,000 to 50,000 mountain lions live in twelve western states (Arizona, California, Colorado, Idaho, Montana, Nevada, New Mexico, Oregon, Texas, Utah, Washington, Wyoming), with a tiny remnant population in Florida and perhaps the Appalachian Mountains. Reported sightings are increasing in the East, but there are still no verified cougar populations there.

The adaptable cat will live in nearly any habitat that offers space, prey, and good hunting cover, including forests and wood-lands, swamps, and deserts. Lions spread themselves out thinly and are generally solitary, except for mothers with kittens. A male usually claims a home range that includes the territories of several females. In her book *Mountain Lion: An Unnatural History of Pumas and People*, contributor Chris Bolgiano reports that lion researchers have found that daughters often live close to mothers and that mothers and daughters occasionally meet and even hunt together long after the daughters have struck out on their own.

The size and exclusivity of an individual's territory varies widely. In British Columbia a male's territory may encompass 57 square miles, while a cat in the sparer habitats of Nevada may claim 140 square miles. Some biologists have come to believe that under natural conditions lions regulate their own populations based more on their desire to maintain a certain distance from one another rather than on the availability of prey. In other words, the habitat could support more lions than the lions them-selves allow. Males kill other males and may also kill females, although they generally don't kill females with whom they have mated. They won't kill their own young if the mother is present, but male lions will kill unattended kittens.

Tom cats range widely, rarely spending more than one day in the same location. They hunt almost constantly and are always on the lookout for females in heat. Mature females generally prefer to stay in more familiar territory, where they know what resources are available for raising young, but both males and females will redefine their territories in response to stronger interlopers or the death of a neighboring lion. Although a lion's senses of sight and hearing are better than its sense of smell, individuals mark their territories with scent, often scraping up little piles of dirt to top with scat or urine.

No lasting bond is established between a male and female, but a breeding pair may hunt and travel together for a week or two. Females yowl during estrus, and cougars also reportedly whistle, meow, chirp, purr, caterwaul, growl, hiss, and scream.

Females typically breed every other year. In some areas, cougar reproductive cycles appear to be timed so kittens are born when deer are fawning; the doe's misfortune means survival for the lion's brood. The female chooses a den in a concealed, sheltered spot, such as a shallow cave, under a rock ledge, or in a heavy thicket. After a gestation period of eighty-eight to ninety-seven days, the female gives birth to one to six kittens (the average is two to three), which are born blind and covered with soft brown fur with black spots. Their eyes open after about ten days and they're weaned at about two months of age. At first, the female leaves her young for a couple of days at a time in a protected place while she ventures out to hunt. When the cubs are big enough, she begins taking them along on short excursions. The mother teaches her offspring how to hunt and how to avoid life's dangers, and as the kittens grow the family ranges farther. By the time the kittens are eighteen to twenty-two months old, they've covered the mother's entire territory and are ready to disperse. Mortality rates for kittens up to this age of independence is 20 to 30 percent. (In captivity, cougars have lived for eighteen

years, though life in the wild is probably not as long.) Siblings
may stay together for several months or longer before striking
out on their own to look for vacant territories, sometimes 75 to
100 miles from their birthplace. As habitat has become more
fragmented, it's hard for cats—especially dispersing juveniles—
to travel without crossing paths with humans. These inexperienced adolescents are frequently the lions who get into trouble,
stealing unsupervised dogs and cats and showing up in school-
yards. In this section of *Shadow Cat*, Elizabeth Marshall Thomas
thinks like a cat in "Path of the Puma," as she explores what
might draw a cougar into town.

We've learned a great deal about *Felis concolor* since
Hornocker first tackled the American lion. And we are seeing
more of them—without having to travel to such places as the
River of No Return. Lions are in our backyards and we are in
theirs. Urban sprawl, the increased popularity of outdoor recreation, and our growing ecological inquisitiveness have made it
harder for mountain lions to maintain a comfortable distance.

If we're going to live with lions, it's important to know their
natural history. How many deer do they eat? How many dogs
and sheep? How consistently do they regulate their own populations? Just how adaptable are they? Biologists and naturalists,
including the contributors to this section, are asking and answer-
ing such questions.

But even as the questions are answered, a sense of wonder
remains. In his book *Soul Among Lions*, noted researcher and
Shadow Cat contributor Harley Shaw muses, "Consider the beast
that lives on the land, feeds itself by killing the fleetest of animals
without using any weapons, and survives the severest of weather
without any of the technological crutches we see as necessities. In
the niche of the lion, we are not its superior, and it deserves a certain awe." That awe only deepens with the understanding that
the cougar's grace, power, and elusiveness symbolize a wild
province we can never really know.

Mountain Lion

by Susan J. Tweit

León
Felis concolor

Name: Mountain lions are also called cougar and puma; the former is an Andean name, the latter an Amazonian name. *León* in Spanish simply means "the lion." *Felis* is Latin for "cat"; *concolor* is Latin for "one color," referring to the tawny coloring of these big cats.

Size: Up to seven feet from nose to tip of tail; males weigh up to 160 pounds, females to 130 pounds.

Color: Tawny yellow above, belly whitish, tail black at tip; young spotted with black.

Voice: Purrs, hisses, meows, and screams like a mating tom cat.
Range: Wild country throughout the Americas, from Patagonia to the Yukon.
Habitat: Variable over its wide range; includes desert mountains, mesas, swamps.
Notes: Mountain lions' eyes shine green in lights at night.

Early one August morning, a mountain lion was sighted in a suburb at the edge of my desert town. A homeowner called the police, who called the Game and Fish Department. By the time the officers arrived to search for it, all that remained were oversized cat tracks and scared dogs. The lion itself had vanished up an arroyo toward the nearby mountains.

Mountain lions are the soul of the Southwest's desert mountains and mesas. These big cats are secretive and rarely seen, but they make their presence known. The second largest cat in the Americas—only jaguars are larger—*leones* were once the most wide spread wild cat in the Americas, ranging from the tip of South America to northwestern Canada, and from the Pacific coast to the Atlantic. In North America, an all-out war on predators that began with European settlement has eliminated these graceful cats from much of the eastern part of their range. Only where large areas of rugged, relatively inaccessible country remain— including the desert regions—are mountain lions still plentiful.

American folklore is full of stories about *leones*: the blood-curdling screams that they supposedly utter just before they leap on their prey, their sensational ability to kill animals of any size, their penchant for tracking humans. In truth, these big cats are graceful and formidable hunters, but contrary to folklore, they hunt silently. Mountain lions prefer deer, but if deer are scarce, they will kill and eat any available live prey, from elk to calves to poodles to humans. *Leones* hunt like enormous housecats, stalking their prey with tails twitching. The resemblance fades, however, when the big cat puts on the power, rushing forward as fast as forty miles per hour and leaping onto the back of its victim. Once astride its prey, the mountain lion embeds its curving claws in the animal's flesh and bites the victim's neck with its oversized canine teeth, severing the victim's spinal cord with an audible *crack*. *Leones* also hunt by crouching motionless on a cliff ledge or tree branch above a deer trail. When dinner passes underneath, the big cat silently drops on its prey and kills it. Biologists estimate that an adult mountain lion needs to kill the equivalent of one deer a week to survive.

Leones do indeed sometimes stalk humans, and have been known to follow a person's tracks for many miles and never attack him. Recently, however, as people have moved in greater numbers up into the foothills and mesas that are prime *león* territory, human-lion encounters have become more common. In 1991, a mountain lion killed a teenage jogger above Colorado Springs, Colorado. It was the first fatal encounter there in many years. Between 1989 and 1998, half a dozen other people were killed by lions in California, Montana, Colorado, and British Columbia. To put those deaths in perspective, domestic dogs kill, on average, half a dozen people each year in the same region. The best way to avoid a lion attack is to not wander lion country alone. If you do encounter a *león*, say biologists, don't run. Stand your ground, look as big as possible, and make plenty of noise.

Adult *leones* are solitary animals except for the bond between a mother lion and her kittens, and brief mating liaisons. Males sleep around, staying with a given female only for the duration of her estrus. About three months after conception, female mountain lions give birth to two or three kittens in a sheltered place—for instance, an oak thicket, a brushy rockpile, or a shelter cave in a cliff.

Like all cats, young *leones* are born helpless, with their eyes shut tight. By the time they are two months old, however, they have begun to eat meat and to follow their mother to food. In fact, their mother may leave them at a fresh kill for several days while she hunts for their next meal. Mountain lions normally disguise their food by kicking dirt, leaves, and other debris atop the carcass. Still, kills attract other lions, as well as coyotes, ravens, vultures, and eagles. In *Soul Among Lions*, biologist Harley Shaw wonders how the kittens keep from becoming meals themselves while their mother is away. They clearly hide some of the time, but they play too, says Shaw. "Kittens seem to have a glorious time at kills," he writes. "Kill sites with kittens present take on a distinctive appearance—that of a minor tornado." The kittens gnaw every bit of bone into small pieces, reports Shaw, and tear up and scatter the hide, ears, and tail of the carcass in a way that suggests they were used as toys.

Mountain lion families drift apart when the young are eighteen months to two years old. The young *leones* gradually hunt farther and farther from their mother, and finally wander on their own in search of a territory. Depending upon the density of their prey, mountain lions in the Southwest require forty to eighty square miles of landscape. Males must find an unoccupied chunk of suitable territory, or challenge a resident male for possession. Young males and oldsters often wander, homeless, poaching food from occupied territories, until they find a niche or die. Females are less territorial; in fact, their domains often overlap. Biologists say that most of the "problem" *leones*, the killers of people, pets, and livestock, are young males between eighteen months and three years old straying beyond the bounds of the usual lion habitat as they search for their own space.

Bans on mountain lion hunting in several western states and booming deer populations have caused *león* populations to swell in the past two decades. At the same time, human populations have grown as well. Cities and towns have mushroomed, expanding into traditional lion territory. The resultant collision has been deadly for lions. In 1995, 120 "nuisance" lions were shot in California, 67 in Oregon, 60 in Montana, and 17 in Utah. If we insist on living in lion country, we must either learn to accept mountain lions' deadly potential—and the risk to our lives and those of our pets and livestock—or we will lock ourselves into a bitter war for space. If we win that war, we will lose *leones*—an outcome that would impoverish us all.

The Lion's
Silent Return

by Ted Williams

America's mountain lion has staged an amazing comeback—
no thanks to us.

Our lion was up on Hardscrabble Ridge a good half-mile
from the den site, proclaimed Ken Logan's radio receiver. So
today, July 18, 1994, we could safely try for her cubs. The week
before, Logan and his assistant, Jeff Augustine, had backed off in
a hurry when the sleek, healthy eighty-pounder—F-91, as they
call her—had perked her ears forward, hissed, and angled
toward them. Few of the world's large carnivores are less dangerous to our species than the mountain lion—*Felis concolor* (cat
of one color), alias cougar, catamount, puma, panther, painter.

But the ground rules change when you barge into its den, grab nursing cubs, fit them with radio collars, and start punching holes in their ears.

As lion habitat, New Mexico's San Andres Mountains are right for all the wrong reasons. They are part of the vast White Sands Missile Range, where visitors, especially the press, are carefully herded and controlled. Legalizing my presence in this lovely, accidental wilderness was a brace of military police that flanked me as we ascended the forty-five-degree slope in 100-degree desert heat. Corporal Charles Ray and Specialist Richard Thorp, barely out of their teens and full of Rachel Carson's sense of wonder, told me that Army life had its highs and lows, and that this day in lion country with the scientists of the world-renowned Hornocker Wildlife Institute was the highest of the highs. It pleased me to hear them breathing as hard as I when I stopped to adjust my canteen-crammed day pack and extract a yucca spike that had broken off when it hit my femur.

Hiking, Logan had called our activity. As a proper swamp Yankee, I knew it as rock climbing, but he couldn't have driven me off that mountain with the can of Grizzly Guard pepper spray that dangled from Augustine's belt. I marveled at the beauty of this 750-square-mile chunk of Chihuahuan desert, the biggest left in the United States. Lush in the absence of cows, the southern slopes under the high, limestone-layered peaks bloomed with prickly pear; whitethorn acacia; tall, spindly ocotillos; and muhly grasses greening from recent rain. On flats and northern slopes, blue and side-oats grama were greening too, and everywhere palmetto-shaped yuccas and dense stands of sotol brightened the brown rubble.

The air was sweet and clean, and save for the glint of our truck windshields far below, the wild mountainscape was unstained by human spoor. Once we saw the tracks of an adult male lion, and here and there fresh "scrapes"—subtle depressions in duff and dust that sometimes reeked of urine.

For an hour we glassed the den site. No sign of cubs. Logan, his research partner Linda Sweanor, to whom he is married, and Jeff Augustine descended for a closer look. "She's moved them," said Sweanor. "That's why she's up on Hardscrabble." So we rock-climbed to the new den, sucking wind and water. Once Logan fell, bending his radio antenna.

We got to within fifty feet of F-91, but ledge and junipers hid her from our sight. "She knows we're here," Logan announced. Sweanor crossed the valley to watch from the opposite slope and keep us posted on the walkie-talkie. The cubs were growing swiftly; in a few days they'd be weaned and faster than human sprinters. If we didn't tag them today, there probably wouldn't be another chance.

While we waited, Logan related an earlier adventure with a lion known as F-6. Her cubs had been growing swiftly. Logan had tried to intimidate F-6 by easing toward the den. She had charged. "Her ears were forward and her eyes were just glued on me," he recalled. "There was a mountain mahogany bush in front of me, and I thought, 'As soon as she hits that, she's going to break off.' Well, she just blew through it." Inches from Logan's head—so close he could hear the thin desert air sighing across her rippling flanks—F-6 had veered and gone pumping up the mountain.

We hovered around F-91's new den site for three hours, but she held her turf. "Let's try something," said Logan, grabbing the pepper spray. "Let's ease up on her in a group; maybe we can intimidate her." I picked up a baseball bat–size sotol stalk, eliciting a cheerful "Good idea!" from Augustine. The MPs goggled at each other, but advanced like good soldiers.

No grass stem stirred as F-91 slipped out of her den and ghosted down the southeast fork of Bosque Spring Draw.

The spotted, blue-eyed cubs hissed and growled, scratched our wrists, and bit us through our leather gloves. Piercing their ears for plastic tags and tattoo numbers seemed somewhat less traumatic than piercing the ears of teenage girls. Only F-232 got a radio collar. Like M-233, she had a pink nose. Black-nosed M-234 calmed quickly, sucking water from a baby bottle and laying down his freshly perforated ears in contentment. We left them at the den and ran. And as we moved out, F-91 moved in—America's lion, perceived as lord and vermin, loved and loathed by a confused, ignorant nation.

If Africa's lion is king of beasts, America's is footman to the lost dauphin. A big male might go 220 pounds and measure nine feet, but only if you count his arm-thick tail, which is half the length of his body. Because the hyoid bone, at the base of its tongue, is not flexible, our lion can't even roar—a condition that has earned it the further indignity of being lumped with the "small cats." The only crest it ever adorned was the chicken-coop roof, draped thereon as a freshly ventilated carcass.

The lion of the New World first made it into old-world literature in 1500, when Italian explorer Amerigo Vespucci described one he'd seen on a beach in what is now called Central America. At that time no terrestrial mammal native to the Western Hemisphere was more widely distributed. Lion country covered all of what came to be the first forty-eight states, jutting far into Canada and taking in almost all of South America. Quickly, Europeans set about trying to rectify this fact by declaring all-out war on the species, behavior that flabbergasted the Indians and for which their only explanation was that whites were insane.

By the early 1900s bounties and intense government control programs had nearly eliminated mountain lions from the United States. The conservation movement was young and vibrant, but Americans still believed that there were "bad" animals like mountain lions and "good" animals like deer, and that conservation entailed killing the former on behalf of the latter. Thus the architect of the movement, Theodore Roosevelt, was able to dismiss our lion as an evolutionary error in need of correction by people who cared. "Lord of stealthy murder," he called it.

Through the first three-quarters of the twentieth century, things got steadily worse for *Felis concolor*. Writing in the November 1969 *National Geographic*, Maurice Hornocker— founder of the Hornocker Wildlife Institute and the first scientist to seriously study mountain lions in the field—reported that best estimates put the U.S. population at less than 6,500 and probably falling.

But as deer and elk recovered from unrestricted hunting early in the century, so did the cat that eats them. Today, even with its U.S. range diminished by two-thirds, the mountain lion is still the most widely distributed land mammal native to the Western Hemisphere, and some biologists are saying the United States may have as many as 50,000. "The world's big carnivores aren't doing too well. But our lion is an exception, an amazing success story," says Hornocker. "It has come back without any costly committees or commissions, without any congressional hearings, without any threatened or endangered status." Lions have recovered to the point that people squatting in formerly vacant habitat are feeling unsafe, occasionally with good reason. Of the dozen humans known to have been killed between 1890 and 1994, eight died in the last twenty-three years of that period.

The mountain lion is classified as endangered in Florida, where thirty to fifty animals are known to abide. Elsewhere east of the Mississippi it may have been extirpated as a breeding species. While a few cats have been showing up in the Northeast, it's unclear if they represent a remnant of the eastern subspecies, *Felis concolor couguar*, or if they or their ancestors were dumped by people who had acquired them in, say, Texas, where cubs are legally hawked as pets and/or fodder for canned hunts.

———

"We probably spent four million dollars studying the mountain lion, and all we have proven is that it's a big pussycat and eats meat," boomed the voice on my pocket tape recorder. "In California the do-gooders stopped the lion hunt. Now there are too many." The interview had been with Brub Stone, a board member of the Gila (New Mexico) Fish and Gun Club, and I was replaying it for Maurice Hornocker as we sat at his kitchen table in Sun Valley, Idaho. Hornocker—a fit sixty-three, with youthful blue eyes—roared with laughter, then regaled me with stories of other Brubs he'd offended with facts they didn't want to know: "When I used to go to the outfitter and guide meetings in the sixties, I didn't just wear my bulletproof vest but my bullet-proof shorts. They were out for blood. 'Who was this crazy college kid Fish and Game had hired to find out about these damned vermin? Hell, we know all about them.' They were convinced lions had killed all the deer and elk in Idaho and were eating each other."

Later, when we had moved out onto the deck and were watching wood ducks and brook trout slice silver V's and O's in the obsidian surface of the stream below, Hornocker talked about his early research. He had been informed by wildlife literati that a population study of mountain lions was quite impossible. The beast, they said, was simply too elusive. From 1964 to 1974 he and an assistant chased lions through the rugged, remote River of No Return country of central Idaho, treeing them with dogs and immobilizing them with drugs. In hunting season, when rime ice feathered the mossy boulders along Big Creek and the bull trout were campfire orange, they'd shoot two deer and an elk for food, caching the meat around the 200-square-mile study area, where it would stay frozen through the long, brutal winter. Because radio telemetry had not been perfected, tagged lions had to be tracked, observed, and recaptured.

What Hornocker showed the world about the big pussycat that eats meat is that there can never be "too many." He proved that America's lion controls itself by setting up and guarding enormous territories, and that because it distributes itself so sparsely over the earth, it is incapable of materially affecting healthy prey populations. Armed with this knowledge, every lion state in the West save Texas upgraded the status of *Felis concolor* from varmint to be shot on sight to game to be conserved—or in the case of California, nongame to be preserved. That's what good science can do for wild animals.

But good science doesn't happen much these days in state and federal wildlife agencies. Piñata-like dispersal of funds and rapid turnover of bureaucrats make long-term field research like Hornocker's White Sands lion project next to impossible. As leader of the Cooperative Wildlife Research Unit at the University of Idaho, in Moscow, Hornocker had watched his career slip away in endless meetings, planning sessions, and paper pushing. He was, as he recalls, "writing memos in response to memos asking me to write memos." There wasn't time for much else, least of all good science. So in 1985, he quit and set up his unique nonprofit institute, now with an annual budget of $1.5 million. Currently he has a dozen projects under way in the United States and is studying Amur leopards and Siberian tigers in Russia.

Hornocker is learning that the facts America doesn't want to know about its lion extend way beyond those that merely challenge frontier gospel. In the mid-eighties the institute discovered that mountain lions, which early in the century had been shot and poisoned out of Yellowstone National Park, had slipped back in. Since then one of Hornocker's major goals has been to find out how they will interact with the wolves the government is planning to release there; but he can't get the attention of the Interior Department, which refused his recent request to fund the work even as it asked him to assist in rewriting lion-management plans for the national parks. Money, as the official explanation goes, is tight. Also, Interior officials and some environmentalists don't like the idea of someone poking around the park learning things that might further delay wolf recovery.

But if you want to facilitate real recovery of any species, you need to learn as much as you can about it. Good science is serendipitous; facts that had seemed not worth knowing or politically incorrect turn out to be vital for effective management. In Florida good science has revealed that "panthers" have been isolated not by nature but by human development and that historically they exchanged genes with cats far to the west and north. Now it is clear that this grievously inbred population—which we have perhaps wrongly called a subspecies—cannot be "polluted," as had been argued, by an infusion of new genes. In fact, it cannot *survive* without such an infusion, which now is under way with the introduction of lions from Texas.

When Kerry Murphy, Hornocker's man in the greater Yellowstone ecosystem, learned that five lions had established territories in Paradise Valley, just outside the park, it seemed like a worthless fact obtained at needless cost to lions. Stressing animals by running them with dogs and injecting them with drugs has been criticized as inhumane. But it is kinder than preserving the scientific vacuum in which state and federal resource agencies commonly operate. When the Montana Department of Fish, Wildlife and Parks proposed a sport-hunting quota of five lions for Paradise Valley, Murphy successfully opposed it by showing that such mortality could expunge the species from that part of the study area.

—

Ask Hornocker if lion reintroduction is biologically practicable in upstate New York, northern New England, or the Great Smoky Mountains, and he'll tell you it's a piece of cake. Ask eastern fish-and-game officials, and most will tell you it's impossible. What they really mean is that release of cougars, as they are called in the East, would scandalize the hook-and-bullet lobby, which pays their salaries and which prefers that no quadruped assist in killing the East's overabundant deer.

The origin of the few animals apparently extant in Yankeeland, and indeed their very presence, are facts game managers don't want to know. They claim there's no evidence of cougars even as they resolutely refuse to look for that evidence. Nor are they bestirring themselves to seriously protect habitat. Why the denial mode? If the animals did not originate in Texas or elsewhere in the West, it could mean that the eastern cougar—*Felis concolor couguar*—is not extinct. This is a terrifying thought to managers because, without admitting that the beast still exists, the U.S. Fish and Wildlife Service has listed it as endangered—status that would mandate a budget-smashing recovery plan if ever the eastern cougar appeared in the flesh.

A cougar population sparser than the East's seems to be a goal in Texas. Enthroned on a deer-hunting stand thirty-three miles south of Marfa in November 1989, Larry Martin spied four young female lions padding up a dry creek bed.

In Texas you may kill as many mountain lions as you please whenever you please, so Martin dropped all four. "Happy Hunter," effused the *Marfa Independent*. Less happy about such nineteenth century–style management is Dede Armentrout, in charge of the National Audubon Society's southwest regional office. "We've lost a number of species over several decades because the [Texas] Parks and Wildlife Department didn't manage them," she remarks. "It kept saying, 'We've got plenty; don't worry your pretty little heads.'"

Last year Texas conservationists failed in a legislative effort to control lion killing. Speaking out against the bill in a staff report, Parks and Wildlife revealed that it "believed" lion numbers to be "healthy." This, however, is a belief based not on science but on hearsay. "It is believed that mountain lions must be controlled in the vicinity of the bighorn sheep brood pens," continues the report. But, again, there is no scientific basis for such a conclusion. New Mexico—aberrant among states in possessing the courage to underwrite good science and then act on the facts regardless of who might not want to know them—ceased killing lions on behalf of bighorns, then hired Hornocker to do the White Sands study. Lo and behold, lion predation of bighorns *declined*.

Among the facts Texas Parks and Wildlife officials don't want an ignorant public to know is that they don't know anything about lions either. Accordingly, in the state-owned Big Bend Natural Area, they have commissioned a make-believe study that has been ripped apart by virtually every legitimate lion researcher in the country. They initiated another make-believe study, on state land adjacent to the Big Bend Natural Area, after locals caterwauled about lions killing mule deer. The initial approach was simply to knock off a bunch of lions and watch what happened. "Until a new biologist complained, the department wasn't looking at teeth, sex, age, or even stomach contents," reports Armentrout.

Mountain lion regs in California, where the animals may be killed only when threatening humans or livestock, are as untainted by good science as those in Texas. In the 1970s California set up its own bogus studies, designed to prove that the species was in fine shape and that sport hunting, banned by the legislature in 1971, was salubrious for everyone, especially lions. Governor George Deukmejian announced that he would veto any extension of lion protection. In 1985 he vetoed legislation so weak that even the Sierra Club had withdrawn support, so the preservationists got a statewide referendum on the ballot. Proposition 117 passed in 1990, banning lion hunting and authorizing $30 million a year for habitat acquisition. But the law is a favorite target of conservatives, and its future is uncertain.

When a lion killed and partially devoured a forty-year-old female jogger near Sacramento, hunter-rights zealots puffed and blew about how they'd tried to warn the public. "As predicted by the sportsmen of California," wrote Dan Heal, chairman of the California Sportsmen's Task Force, ". . . unwarranted protection of a predatory animal—the mountain lion—has come full circle with the horrible death of Barbara Schoener." Horrified state assemblyman David Knowles (R-Placerville) promised to introduce a bill that would legalize the hunting of lions. "They actually view us as their food," he intoned.

But as a means of keeping the lions away, hunting is no more effective than clapping one's hands. If the facts were otherwise, there should be no problem in British Columbia, where more than 50 percent of all attacks on the continent occur and where the hunting of lions is so relentless that as many as 208 have been killed in a year.

The astonishing thing about our American lion is not that it is known to have killed a dozen humans between 1890 and the mid-1990s, but that it is known to have killed *only* a dozen humans. With much of our large fauna critically depressed in the late nineteenth century, generations of Americans have grown up believing that interactions between humans and wildlife are weird, unnatural, and to be avoided at any cost. "Remove dense and low-lying vegetation where cougars can hide," warns the *New York Times*. "Install outdoor lighting. . . . Do not hike alone." If it has really come to this, why not also suggest wearing steel trash cans and diving helmets or, safer yet, staying indoors?

It's not the idea of getting killed that undoes us; it's the idea of getting eaten. About fifty herdsmen are gored to death by cattle each year, but as Hornocker says, "You don't see movies entitled *The Night of the Cow*."

———

The best way to avoid confrontations with lions is to give them the space they need. But this, too, is a fact we don't want to know, especially if the developer slapping houses on the foothills is building one for us. So even as lions increase, their future dims.

A viable lion population—defined by biologists as one capable of persisting for 100 years—requires 250 breeding adults of each sex. Numbers vary according to location and prey density, but based on Ken Logan's data from New Mexico, 500 breeding lions need 10,000 square miles. Much easier to ban hunting, buy some land here and there, and keep fragmenting habitat.

Ten thousand square miles, Logan told me as we climbed the abandoned observation tower on Skillet Knob, is thirteen times the size of the San Andres Mountains. But that kind of habitat probably exists in New Mexico. A future for New Mexico's lions will, of course, require sound hunting regulations, which Logan has been asked to help draft. And it will require at least two large safe havens—lion reservoirs the size of the White Sands study area where *Felis concolor* can breed and from which youngsters can disperse.

From the rickety observation platform we gazed out over valleys brown and green, and down and up at eroded peaks washed in purples, reds, and golds—lion country as priceless as the Serengeti. Five miles to our southwest the Chalk Hills hung across a mottled sky; the Mockingbird Mountains rose fifteen miles to our north, the Black Range sixty miles west, the Sacramentos forty miles south. In the dry Tularosa lake bed, thirty miles to our southeast, the gypsum salts that give the missile range its name oozed with reflected heat.

"Blip, blip, blip . . ." said Logan's radio receiver. It was F-90 to the southeast. We found F-147 high in the Mockingbirds. And there was M-46 in the Chalk Hills on a course that had taken him past Bosque Canyon. So he had left the tracks we'd seen on our climb for F-91's cubs. F-183 turned up over in West Bosque Canyon. From White Rock Canyon due north, we picked up the frequency of M-221—a nineteen-month-old subadult unsettled, looking for home range. And here was F-89 moving toward us along a ridge to the east, shadowed by M-210. Probably they were mating.

Logan aimed his receiver southwest toward Hardscrabble Ridge, and we picked up the signals of F-91 and her cub F-232— the one I'd held twenty-four hours earlier. Far below us a sparrow hawk dipped out of a dying updraft. We stayed there a long time, washed by the faint San Andres breeze, turning like compass needles over lodestone, listening to our American lions.

Way out there, with them now, we padded along high ledges, ghosted through rocky draws, flowed over green foothills. We saw and heard and smelled everything in lion country, and all of it that day was beautiful and right.

Path of the Puma

by Elizabeth Marshall Thomas

It seems a regular occurrence these days: accounts in western newspapers of pumas hunting people's dogs and cats, eating pet food left out on people's sun decks, and hiding in the dense, exotic shrubbery that people cultivate in their yards. In 1992 I made a study of the puma sightings that had occurred that year within the city limits of Denver and Boulder and came to the conclusion that the wanderers were young animals, probably off on their own for the first time and not coping well. The lack of a cultural taboo against our species, combined with inexperience and bad judgment, had brought them into the towns. Or so it seemed. In nearly every case, I had no difficulty figuring out where the youngster had come from or why he or she had chosen the place in question. All the places were at the edge of the foothills on the plains, and in all cases, I thought, the youngster, when starting his or her journey, probably would have had no choice but to travel east. West led back into the mountains, where, it seemed fair to conclude, the adult members of the growing puma population had acquired all the good territories. Surely big and powerful pumas already sat in the lookouts and patrolled the boundaries of the numerous Eastern Slope puma habitats and would chase any young newcomer away.

In fact, I could think of only one question that wasn't readily answered by topography combined with human demographics, and that was why the young pumas came so fearlessly straight into the towns when they could have slipped around them. In order to guess at an answer to that question, however, all I needed to do was to go up into the hills and see for myself what the youngsters must have seen as kittens. East of the foothills in the Denver-Boulder area, the Colorado plain is more or less a continuous urban sprawl, thick here, thin there; and from almost anywhere along the Eastern Slope one looks east at a sea of buildings with glittering windows, surrounded by streams of cars. The scene is sufficiently remote that sirens and horns and other urban sounds aren't audible; the scene contains, in short, nothing alarming when viewed by day. But viewed by night, it becomes positively entrancing for members of the cat family. Boulder, for instance, becomes a vast array of lights, some moving, others spinning, still others flashing, a scene so visually appealing to the cat family that it might have been designed just for their pleasure. As housecats watch television, not really caring what the program is about but thrilled by the irregular, jerking movements, so the young pumas in their mothers' lookouts in the Rockies might have viewed the flitting lights below.

The next step for the outward-bound youngster is to start down the mountainside, toward the by now completely familiar landscape, which he or she has been viewing nearly every day and night since emerging from the den. The first human installations the young puma would encounter on the eastward journey would be the widely spaced homes of well-to-do suburbanites, who each year build houses ever higher on the slopes. Since, presumably, the appeal of such neighborhoods is their remoteness and their privacy, the human residents tend to be almost as quiet and as circumspect as the pumas themselves—after ten o'clock at night these neighborhoods are silent and dark, and most people are inside the houses. Often at night I've quietly walked through these neighborhoods just to learn what a puma might encounter, and the answer is: nothing. Needless to say, I wasn't furtive—on the contrary, I walked in the middle of the road. But not one person ever saw me. No one even realized I was there. The dogs knew, of course—once in a while one of them barked, but usually from inside a house. In no case did anyone investigate, and sometimes the people even shushed the dog. So it seems that from the start a passing puma could expect no opposition.

Pumas like paths and follow them whenever possible. They have their own puma corridors, and they also follow our paths, trails, and roads, as well as riverbanks and canyons, much as we would. In consequence, most of the pumas who entered Boulder seemed to have come (or so I thought) along relatively few pathways. An informal and cursory survey yielded four possible routes into town that I thought I could identify: two of the routes came down canyons and two followed the banks of brooks. Each canyon route led into an upscale neighborhood with neon green lawns and a puzzling maze of fences, but the brooks became unkempt, forgotten ditches and thus remained wild-looking even deep inside the city, which was where many of the sightings took place.

In most cases the puma wasn't sighted until afternoon. The people who discovered him usually got excited, in contrast to the young puma himself, who usually remained perfectly calm.

That, too, seemed disconcerting to his discoverers. A puma who shows no fear of people seems sinister, dangerous, especially when the people are so much afraid of him. However, the reason for the puma's calmness could also be surmised by traveling his likely route. Being of a crepuscular species, the puma would most likely start out on a journey sometime in the evening, after resting all day, just as we might start a journey in the morning after resting all night. That timing would bring a traveling puma into the city in the middle of the night, when the streets were empty and all was quiet. If a puma had tried to travel through the city by day, people would have seen him, with the resulting fanfare of police and emergency vehicles, inevitably ending in disaster for the puma.

So the puma surely arrived before dawn and found himself deep inside the city by the time the city woke up. Then, all of a sudden, doors began to open and people and their dogs began to come out. Soon traffic filled the streets and the city was once again alive and busy. Surely the puma was taken aback, and surely he felt he had no choice but to hide as best he could. In the sightings that I investigated, most of the pumas had chosen to hide in bushes or long grass surrounded by open space—the most dramatic example being a puma that hid all day on the grounds of the school where my grandson, David, was attending seventh grade. From afar, that particular school must have looked wonderful to the young puma—set against a hill too steep for building, the school is surrounded by fields where the grass is long and golden, like wild grass. Best of all, a tangle of bushes grows at the edge of these fields. Hidden in these bushes, the young puma could watch the doings of all the people while hoping that none came too near or threatened him. After a day of watching warily as children swarmed around him, playing soccer and generally making lots of noise, he must have lost most of his fear just through acclimatization, and when in the afternoon someone noticed him, perhaps because he got up for a drink or to move into the shade, he had undergone about ten hours of city life during which nothing bad had happened to him. By then the busy school ground must have seemed somewhat less scary. Such was not the experience of his astonished discoverer, however, who probably had never before given much thought to pumas. No wonder the man was frightened when an enormous tawny cat calmly appeared from nowhere on the school ground.

I didn't learn what happened to that particular puma. Possibly he was killed by the wildlife officers or by the police, although the attitude of the Boulder citizens is so favorable to pumas and, in fact, to most wildlife that the policy of the Colorado Division of Wildlife is to tranquilize the pumas and transport them back to the hills. Even so, the Division justifiably fears lawsuits and undoubtedly has to kill many straying pumas simply because of the vast number of litigious people who would view any encounter as a bonanza and sue the state.

Fear of lawsuits sealed the fate of a young puma who, in August 1992, somehow got himself into the heart of Denver. He had followed a dwindling watercourse to the intersection of Hampton and Monaco, two swarming thoroughfares lined with shopping malls and roaring with traffic. A worse place for a puma can scarcely be imagined. Even so, early one morning he entered a neighborhood next to these streets and hid there until eight o'clock at night, when a dog saw him and chased him up a tree. He had probably been trying to resume his journey. When the owners of the tree saw why their dog was barking, they called the police. With the police came firefighters, reporters, an entire television crew with vans, cables, lights, and cameras, and, eventually, an officer from the Division of Wildlife. The excitement drew a large crowd of passersby, who, much taken with the sight of the young puma peering down at them, begged the authorities to spare his life. The wildlife officer wanted to tranquilize the puma and move him out of town, but when the dart hit the youngster, he panicked and jumped out of the tree in a dash for freedom. The police opened fire and killed him.

He must have seemed enormous, at least to some of the reporters present. An early edition of one of the papers gave his weight at 250 pounds. In fact, he was hardly more than a kitten, and in his starved condition probably weighed between 60 and 70 pounds. A photo in another paper shows him lying dead, his gaunt little body curled at the feet of the district wildlife officer.

After this sad drama appeared on the local television news, some people chose not to report sightings lest other pumas suffer the same fate. Such was the decision of a young couple in Boulder late one night when their dog, Bailey, chased a young puma up onto the roof of a toolshed. I met these people while investigating another sighting in the same neighborhood, and they told me that when they saw the puma looking down at the dog, they assumed it was trying to hunt him. In this they were surely mistaken. If, in fact, the puma behaved as they described—they said it had crouched on the roof for fifteen or twenty minutes looking down—it had been treed by Bailey and was afraid, nothing else. Yet, even believing as they did, the young people were generous to the puma and did not call the police. Instead, they brought Bailey inside and left the puma alone. In the morning, it was gone, perhaps headed back to the hills, and no harm was done.

Are pumas dangerous? Some are and some aren't. The pumas who find their way into cities have so far hurt no one, although dogs, cats, and chickens have evidently fallen victim to some of them. Even so, pumas do attack people. Pumas look for all the world like exceptionally beautiful housecats, so it is hard to believe that harm could come of them. Yet the fact that people are almost exactly the same size as deer cannot be lost on pumas. In other words, people are the perfect size to be prey, just as voles are exactly the right size for housecats, and attacks do take place. One June day, two pumas attacked a Boulder woman, after which one of them may have moved on to attack a young man. The Boulder *Daily Camera* of June 4, 1990, reports the first event, telling of the young woman who, while jogging in the hills near the city, saw a puma crouch low and come toward her. She threw a stone, but the puma kept coming. At that point, the woman noticed a second puma creeping up on her from behind, so, with great presence of mind, she made her way up an embankment and climbed a tree at the top. On her way up the tree, she felt pain in the calf of her leg, and looking down she saw that the pumas were climbing after her, one behind the other. The nearer of the two, the one who had scratched her, was looking up at her with its paw on her branch.

At this point, according to the *Camera*, the woman expected the pumas to kill her. However, refusing to give up without a fight, she stomped on the head of the nearest puma. That puma dropped to the ground. The other puma then climbed higher, snarling at her as she tried to drive it back with a branch. Eventually, though, the second puma also dropped to the ground. For a while the two paced back and forth under the tree; then they went off to drink from a stream and finally disappeared for good. The courageous young woman climbed down from the tree and ran a quarter of a mile to a group of houses.

A few weeks later, about twenty-five miles away, a puma who might have been one of the young woman's attackers killed a young man. He, too, had been jogging at the time of the attack, which came from behind. Searchers found his partly eaten body a short distance from the road; he had been dragged there and then covered with leaves by the puma as if he had been a deer. Eventually the searchers noticed a puma crouched at a distance, watching them. Later, this puma was hunted down and killed. It was a young male, about two years old, weighing about 100 pounds. His stomach contained fragments of the young man's body, proving that the hunters had found the right animal and that a man-eater did not remain at large.

Attacks on human beings by pumas were studied by Dr. Paul
Beier from the University of California, who presented his find-
ings at a conference on pumas sponsored by the Colorado
Division of Wildlife in Denver in 1991. His study examined fifty
unprovoked attacks that had taken place in twelve western states
and in two Canadian provinces over the past 100 years. The most
astonishing attack happened on Vancouver Island, which in
itself was interesting, since the pumas of Vancouver seem more
inclined to attack people than pumas anywhere else, suggesting,
once again, a cultural bent. Also significant is that the inclination
refutes a generally held belief that pumas are less bold where
they are hunted. On Vancouver, pumas are heavily hunted by
sportsmen, yet the pumas there are said to be very bold indeed,
and Vancouver continues to be the scene of an ongoing series of
puma attacks on human beings. What, if anything, hunting has
to do with this is unclear.

In the Vancouver attack, a puma jumped through the large
glass window of an isolated cabin, knocking over the only
lantern and seizing the cabin's owner, a telephone linesman who
was preparing for bed and had undressed to his underwear. In
the dark the brave man, with the puma biting him, fought his
way into his kitchen, where he got a knife and stabbed the puma
until it let him go. Running outside, he slammed the door
behind him, closing the wounded puma inside and himself outside on a bitter winter night in the snow. Although badly
injured, the nearly naked man got into his boat and rowed six
miles against a strong wind and a heavy sea to a neighbor's cabin,
where, since no one was at home, he broke in. By then close to
death from shock and hypothermia, he had to huddle under a
blanket for several hours before he could dial the telephone. His
rescuers found and shot the puma, who was still locked in the
cabin. Like most other pumas who have attacked people, this
one was a young male.

Of the fifty unprovoked attacks discussed by Dr. Beier,

two-thirds were made on children. In eleven cases the child was alone, but in sixteen cases other children were present, and in eight cases an adult was present, all of which reinforces the notion that the size and age of the intended victim, rather than the presence or absence of another person, were significant to the puma.

—

One result of the conference in Denver was that a sort of protocol was endorsed to encourage people to make their property less hospitable to pumas. Homeowners were advised to eliminate hiding places by cutting back their shrubbery, and to eliminate sources of food by bringing pets inside at night and not feeding the deer. Hikers were told of a canned pepper spray to be aimed at the face of an attacking puma but were warned against spraying into the wind, which could leave the hikers thrashing helplessly on the ground, unable to see or hear, right in front of the advancing puma. (When I tested a can, the product malfunctioned, letting fall a drop or two of peppery juice on my feet. What a disappointment that would have been if I had been trying to deter a puma!) More reliable methods for repelling puma attacks make use of the fact that pumas are sometimes susceptible to a display of force. If attacked, one might shout in a deep voice or make threatening gestures or brandish a stick. The key word here is *sometimes*, and the point is illustrated by the experience of a hiker who, against park regulations, had unleashed her miniature terrier at the head of a trail that led down a narrow canyon with steep walls. As the two entered the canyon—the dog first, the woman second—a puma, who evidently had been watching them from a ledge on the canyon wall, suddenly plopped down in front of them. The brave dog flew at the puma, who seemed aghast and fled along the trail with the terrier at his heels, demonstrating that even a tiny creature can route a puma by showing some convincing aggression.

On the other hand, one shouldn't count on it. Rethinking the situation even as he fled, the puma suddenly spun around, seized the terrier, and leaped up the canyon wall with the dog in his mouth. Neither was ever seen again.

Of course, the more people present, the better the chance of spotting the attacking cat in the first place. Like most man-eating leopards and tigers who attempt to prey upon human beings, man-hunting pumas tend to attack from behind, with a bite to the back of the neck. According to Dr. Beier's survey, most people who were attacked by a puma and lived to tell the story reported that they never knew what was happening until they felt the terrible thump of its body, and then the teeth and claws.

Even so, some people were able to fight off the puma. According to Dr. Beier's survey, of the thirty-five children who were attacked, nine were alone and were killed, but the others were saved because someone else saw what was happening and came to the rescue. Also according to the survey, once the puma had launched its attack, fighting back turned out to be an effective form of defense. Playing dead, which seems to help people when attacked by bears, was strongly contraindicated in a puma attack, as the deception could result in the victim's being dragged to a more private location, with fatal consequences. After all, the bear's aggression often results from its fear of the human being, who allays that fear by assuming a nonthreatening posture. The cat, in contrast, may be looking for a meal, and would find a nonthreatening posture inviting. When attacked by a cat, it would be much better to do what bears themselves do in tiger country—stand up tall and face the attacker. One might stare at the cat's eyes and shout "Bad puma!" or "Back off!" in a deep, menacing voice while brandishing something—one's jacket, say, or one's camera. The cat is only trying to eat, after all, and doesn't want trouble. But don't stoop down to get a stick or a rock— children and crouching people are the most frequent victims of puma attacks. Why so? Because most hunting, or hunting in the old way, is pragmatic food-gathering behavior and is best done carefully and wisely. Hunting for food (a different activity than hunting for sport) lacks the aggression that drives reckless, war-like behavior. One of the primary rules of hunting for food, at least for the animals and people who live in the old way, is simply this: be careful, tackle only what you think you can handle, and above all don't get hurt.

—

One of Dr. Beier's accounts of escape from pumas brought much laughter and even derision from the audience, as if he had intended the story as humor, which as far as I could tell he had not. I repeat the story here because of its implications and because, to me, it is the most intriguing of all the accounts. A woman who was backpacking alone on a remote trail was attacked by a puma. In the usual way, the puma leaped on the woman from behind, grabbing her by the pack and knocking her down. But she twisted herself around in her pack straps and kept the pack between herself and him. Face to face with her attacker, she spoke smoothly and encouragingly. Although he had her in his power and could have killed her at any time, he instead was willing to listen to her. Eventually, other hikers came along the trail and drove him away. Why did this amuse some members of Dr. Beier's audience? Perhaps because the concept of making an emotional or intellectual connection with a puma at such a moment was remote from their experience, and they were unable to see themselves in a similar situation, to make the leap.

"Nice kitty," some people joked, as if they thought that the puma had attacked because he was angry and that the woman had managed to placate him.

In fact, something very different was probably the case. Probably the woman's voice and demeanor had taken the puma by surprise, so that his hunt metamorphosed into a different kind of encounter, requiring different behavior. He must have been wondering what that behavior should be, and in hopes of getting more information kept watching and listening.

After all, any intelligent, empathetic social being must often make decisions about his or her relationship to another being. Is the other being a friend or a foe or a meal? Because cats are creatures of the edge, dependent entirely upon animal protein, they usually select the third option, even to the point of occasional, opportunistic cannibalism. But they don't always select the third option. The puma had been sensitive enough to see that the woman didn't act like meat.

The men and women of Dr. Beier's audience, mocking suburbanites who typically interact with the natural world only by occasionally going hiking or hunting or camping, were very far removed from this kind of dilemma. But the puma was not. Nor, evidently, was the woman. And at one time, when our kind lived in the old way, as wild animals still live today, neither were we.

Read in Tooth
and Claw

by M. Cathy Nowak

When I was young, I heard, somewhere, the line from Tennyson about "nature, read in tooth and claw." It was not until many years later when, as an adult, I saw the passage in print that I realized the quote was actually ". . . red in tooth and claw," a reference to the color of blood. I prefer my original, childish interpretation. Through it, I saw the designs of nature exposed in the power and need of the predator. It allowed me to read the story of nature free of the value judgments implicit in the image of blood dripping from fangs and talons. Nature makes no value judgments, it acts only on need: the need for shelter, space, reproduction, and food. It is in satisfying its need for food that the mountain lion has gained my admiration and respect.

Mountain lions, like all cats, are "obligate carnivores"; they must eat meat. While their competitors, such as wolves, bears, and coyotes, can supplement their diets with plant material, the cougar must regularly find and kill animal prey to survive. In response to this need, they have, through the ages, become very good at what they do. Deer, the North American cougar's usual prey, are larger than the cats themselves, requiring stealth to approach and skill and power to overcome. I admire cougars' efficiency at taking these large prey and their economy in using the harvest and keeping it from others, or at least trying to. I am also intrigued by the apparent contradiction between the swift, silent killer and the tender, attentive parent that is a female mountain lion.

I have examined kills made by mountain lions, sometimes within hours of the attack, and attempted to read the story of the kill in the signs that are left. When the kill is made in snow, the story can be as easy to read as the pages of an illustrated book. At times, however, it can be like trying to read an unfamiliar language or a code you are not meant to understand. Lions locate prey by hunting: intentionally moving through the forest or brush looking for a meal. But they also find prey incidental to other activities. For example, a female and her single kitten are moving through the woods and stop to rest. While the female contentedly nurses her young, a small band of deer walk by about forty yards away. The cat is up and stalking in a single fluid motion. Within ten yards she is running, bounding through the snow, extending her claws for traction as she turns and anticipates the response of the prey. A frightened fawn turns away from the group and the cougar turns with it, almost certain now of success. She reaches the fawn at the base of a large tree where the end is swift and I, later in the day, read the story in the snow. The story is a short one, as are most of them, the entire drama having taken less than thirty seconds to unfold.

Regardless of how a mountain lion locates its prey, the chase is usually short. Cougars are short-winded and use rocks, brush, and other cover to stalk close before giving chase. Few people have seen a wild cougar attack its intended prey, but based on the reports of those who have, and on examinations of the results of the attacks, it seems that cougars use several different methods for making a kill. In some cases, the cat leaps onto the back of the deer and either bites through the back of the neck, severing the spinal cord, or uses its large forepaw and sharp claws to pull the head around and back, breaking the neck. Another, and perhaps the most impressive, method is to jump at the prey, striking it in the neck or shoulders with such force that the prey is driven to the ground. The cat can then bite the throat and strangle the victim. There are undoubtedly other methods and individual variations on all techniques, but, with the possible exception of inexperienced young mountain lions, the kill is invariably quick, quiet, and clean.

On a warm Saturday afternoon in August, as I attempted to locate a female cougar I was tracking, her radio signal intensified in spite of the fact that I was standing still. Just as I determined the direction the cat was coming from and that she was, indeed, coming toward me, a deer snorted and bolted from the brush in front of me. The deer was wide-eyed and in a hurry. Within seconds, another deer came from the same patch of brush, intending to escape through the space I was occupying. She turned abruptly when she saw me and passed through the same opening used by the first deer. I stood, watching and listening. The telemetry could do little to tell me where the cat was, since at this close range the power of the signal completely swamped the receiver. I held my pepper spray ready although it, too, would be of little use; if the cat mistook me for a deer in that heavy brush, I would have no time to use it.

A third deer appeared to my right, sneaking slowly through the brush. Her eyes were wide, looking for the slightest movement.

Her ears stretched forward, reaching for any sound to hint at the direction of danger. Her body was taut with tension as she stepped out in front of me. I could have touched her shoulder from where I stood, transfixed. It seemed, for a second, that all the forest was holding its breath. Then she turned and saw me. She stamped in alarm at this unexpected danger and bounded away. Her flight from me took her right into the path of the silent, stalking mountain lion. As she landed her second leap, I could see only her head above the brush as the lion struck. Her head jerked around to the side, but whether from reflex or impact I will never know. She bawled and dropped out of sight behind some brush. I dropped to a crouch behind the suddenly insignificant barrier of shrubs, more frightened than I had ever been in the presence of a cougar. I listened to the quiet sounds of the deer's last movements and of the cat moving around on the prey, adjusting her grip and catching her breath. Ten minutes passed before the cougar moved her prey to a more secure location to feed, and called to her kittens. Only then, with the cat occupied with her young, did I mark my location and sneak out of the woods. I had been within fifty feet of a cougar making a kill and I was in awe. I had neither seen nor heard the lion itself, but there was absolutely no question that she was there. She and her kittens would eat that day, and my already powerful respect for the ghost cat had been fattened as well.

Little is known about the success rate of hunting cougars, but I suspect they miss many more meals than they catch. Perhaps it is for this reason that I saw so little waste by the cats I studied. It is just plain easier to eat what is already on the ground than to expend energy and risk injury to catch something new. Mountain lions often go to great pains to preserve their prey from the ravages of heat, insects, and scavengers, both furred and feathered. I have seen evidence of a cat dragging her prey 100 yards from the site of the kill, under an open patch of very large pine trees, to complete seclusion in a patch of small pines with outer branches that hung to the ground. Once the cat has moved the kill to a secure location and fed, it will usually cover it, or at least the portion fed upon, with pine needles, leaves, sticks, grass, soil, snow, or whatever is available at the site. Lacking any other choices, cougars may cover kills with the hair of the prey itself, plucked from the hide in preparation to feed.

While we cannot know the lion's motivation for moving and covering the kill, these behaviors serve several valuable functions in preservation of the meat. Moving the prey to the cover of the trees keeps it shaded from the heat and desiccation of the sun and also hides it from the searching eyes of scavenging birds such as ravens, vultures, and magpies. Covering the kill with vegetation, soil, or snow serves to insulate it from the day's heat and dampen the scent emitted by the carcass. Ground-coursing scavengers such as coyotes, bears, and badgers have acute senses of smell, so their noses as well as their eyes must be fooled. Flies, too, are foiled by the covering of the kill. The layer of debris makes it difficult, sometimes impossible, for flies to reach the opened carcass to lay their eggs. This reduces the hatch of maggots and slows decomposition. Lions exhibit another behavior at some kills that both amazes and baffles me. They will sometimes remove the rumen from the carcass and bury it at some distance from the rest of the kill. The rumen is the deer's stomach, where bacteria help to digest the deer's otherwise indigestible food; it is a virtual fermentation vat. The advantage of removing it may be that it slows bacterial contamination of the meat, thereby slowing spoilage. What I don't understand is what motivates the cats in this behavior. Maybe they simply find the smell offensive and try to remove it from their feeding place. Whatever the motivation and whatever the effect, it is a delicate operation. To break open the rumen as it is poised over the kill could ruin the day for lion and researcher alike.

Biologists and hunters have often reported incidents of waste by cougars: kills that were briefly fed upon and then left to rot.

The myriad scavengers undoubtedly find these kills to be a boon, but the lions I studied never gave them such a gift. They returned to their kills night after night to feed until there was nothing left to feed on. In the spring, I found a nine-month-old elk calf that had been killed the day before by a female with three kittens. On my first rainy day arrival to the site, I saw the family of four sleeping in a heap under a sheltering tree. They had fed well and they slept reassured, no doubt, by each other's presence. They reminded me of stuffed animals hastily tossed in a pile against a pillow. From my vantage, I could not tell which lion part belonged to which lion. That day I let sleeping cats lie and returned the next day to find the kill. The family was bedded some 300 yards from it, a far-enough distance for me to examine the prey. For eight days the lions used the same bed by day and returned to the kill to feed at night. The weather was cool, even bringing snow one night and, with it, tracks of the mother and three romping, playful young. I visited the kill each day during this time to document their feeding. When the cats left the area, the kill had been reduced to bones and hide. The coyotes wouldn't get much from this one. I wonder if, in some of those reported cases of waste, the cat wasn't just sleeping away the daylight hours somewhere else, returning to the kill after dark unseen and unjudged.

A female with kittens will often bed far from her kill. Mountain lion kittens are very vulnerable, especially during the first few months of life, and kills attract the very animals that pose the greatest threat: coyotes, bears, eagles, badgers, wolverines, and other mountain lions. It makes sense for the female to keep her young secure and away from these dangers. At first she will leave the kittens in the den while she travels to her kill to feed, but as they grow older, they will travel with her to the prey. Before dawn, they will all return to the bed site. These treks can be long and tiring for short legs. Following the tracks of one family's hike to their food cache, I found that they had stopped to rest about halfway to their goal and again about halfway home. I often wonder if the kittens are able to eat enough at the kill to make up for the energy spent in getting there, but the security of sleeping the day away in a safe place must make the trip worthwhile.

As I stand and read the snow, I think of how the mountain lion has shaped the story of these woods. All others who live here are influenced, in some way, by the power, need, and presence of these great cats. To the lion is owed the wariness of the deer; speed is of little help against a danger undiscovered. The best hope of smaller prey is to remain secret and unseen. But if the cat gives chase, they might escape into a hole too small for the predator to follow. There are times when small size is an advantage. Even birds, with the gift of flight, must beware the cougar. Small birds foraging on the ground, fooled by a seemingly sleeping cat, can be snatched up as what would seem to be hardly a snack for a lion. Bears supplement their poor spring diet with kills usurped from cougars. Wolves, too, enjoy the bounty provided by a skillful cat. The other scavengers of lion kills do well to pay attention as they feed so that they do not become cougar food themselves. For the most part, all have adapted to the presence of the mountain lion. Those that are unwary, slow, far from a hole, or fooled by apparent slumber will be taken by the swift, silent hunter as, with tooth and claw, she continues to forge the nature of these woods.

II. Tales of the Cat:
Encounters

Tracks in mud, in snow, or baked into the packed dirt of a mountain trail; rustling in the brush; the sound of claws on bark; an eerie cry in the night. A glimpse of long golden tail and muscled shoulders. The presence of an animal felt but unseen. The cougar's stealth and strength make for powerful storytelling.

The mountain lion's aliases alone evoke stories: catamount ("cat of the mountain"), king cat, swamp screamer, devil cat, ghost cat, shadow cat. The Cherokee called the cougar Klandagi, "Lord of the Forest." Indians of Puget Sound called him "Fire Cat." To the Cree he was Katalgar, "Greatest of Wild Hunters." The Chickasaw called the cougar Ko-licto, "Cat of God."

Leaders of some Pueblo hunting societies were called Cougar Men, and other North American tribes wrapped their newborn sons in cougar skins and made their arrow quivers from the pelts, hoping to absorb the magic. In 1894, American zoologist William T. Hornaday wrote, "Let me give him one more name, and call him the Story Lion! Owing to his size, agility, alleged fierceness, and very wide geographical distribution, he is the storyteller's animal par excellence."

As the distinction between wild and settled places blurs, cougar sightings increase. Encounters with the cats become more problematic and in many ways stranger, giving rise to disconcerting, beguiling, and dramatic tales. The mountain lion's reality has changed over the past twenty years, so we thought it important to present stories that would reflect this altered landscape.

In the past decade mountain lions have made themselves apparent in disturbing ways and in unexpected places: in a schoolyard in the suburbs of Portland, Oregon; alongside a kindergarten class on a field trip in Montana; on an Idaho golf course; in neighborhood backyards; on well-worn hiking trails in California and Colorado. All of these sightings—as do many of the stories in this section—point to the question of habitat. In his book *The Ecology of Fear*, Mike Davis notes that the Los Angeles area may be home to more mountain lions than Yellowstone.

These stories take us from the wooded hills of northern California and forests of Montana to the Malpai borderlands and high deserts of the Four Corners region, and from the mountains of West Virginia to the Sierras. All raise questions of home, of independence, and of a longing and need for wild and open spaces. They are stories of tracking and imagining, and of glimpses of this elusive predator.

The mountain lion is an animal more often not seen than seen—as many of these stories attest. Yet the animal's presence, once sensed, is palpable and powerful. It is an animal that is as fearsome as it is alluring. We want to see one, yet we are terrified of doing so. We are afraid, yet often mesmerized in its presence. We have encroached on the cougar's territory, and influenced its habits with ours. We hunt it, yet seek to protect it.

Tales of cats almost seen, never seen, of frightening or inspiring encounters—in this section we gather contemporary accounts of encounters with mountain lions that illustrate our current, troubled relationship with the ghost cat.

On Not Encountering
an Eastern Panther

by Chris Bolgiano

Sometimes it seems that I am the only person I know who hasn't seen a panther in the mountains of western Virginia, where I live. Reports come in from all sides. Lori saw a black one playing at the foot of Little North Mountain not far from here, but she is a poet and a writer of fantasy novels, and sees things in the shadows that other people don't. My neighbor Willy was startled the other night by a big, long-tailed cat that ran in front of his car; he is a hunter and said he never saw anything like it in the woods, but it was night and he barely got a glimpse as the animal streaked by. David saw one on the outskirts of the small city down in the valley where he lives, but he is, sadly, too often in his cups. Gil was riding his mountain bike just across the state line in West Virginia and swears he saw one gliding through the green gloom, but he runs a bike touring company, and if tales of eastern panthers spark up his clients' experience, so much the better. Dave is a self-taught woodsman who lives what is called an alternative lifestyle, and he is convinced that the eyeshine and yowling beside his campfire one night was a cougar, though he couldn't find any sign. Larry watched a mother and kitten in his rifle scope for several minutes one brilliant autumn afternoon while he was squirrel hunting. He is a professional biologist, and his story is not easily discounted.

The cat that easterners call panther, painter, or catamount was officially extirpated by 1938, when the last wild cougar was shot in Maine, but sightings have never ceased. Sparse and scattered in the early twentieth century, by the last quarter of it cougar sightings swelled to such a volume that they became a phenomenon in themselves. Of the thousands of people who have reported a sighting in recent decades, a handful found the experience powerful enough that it changed their lives. A glimpse of rippling cat muscle and long, low, curving tail charged their view of the world with a new kind of emotional, if not spiritual, energy. Afterward they dedicated themselves to collecting other sightings, interviewing the sighters, and searching for field evidence to confirm the existence of the great cats. They are sane people, as far as I can tell, and invariably kind and friendly. There is about them a definite aura of the outcast as well as an unquestioning faith. If they had a leader, they might qualify as some sort of harmless cult. The eastern cougar has become a mythic presence. I cast my mind in search of it, as I walk through my 100 acres of woods along the flank of Cross Mountain.

Until the 1990s, state and federal wildlife officials routinely dismissed eastern cougar sightings. People who reported seeing cougars were often subjected to rude treatment as cranks or drunks. There's no telling what good evidence was trashed by closed-minded bureaucrats unwilling to take the risk that cougars might actually be there. Finding cougars would mean some unpleasant work for public wildlife agencies. The eastern cougar subspecies is listed on the federal Threatened and Endangered Species List (as *Felis concolor couguar*), giving it certain protections, at least on federal land. Agency officials would need to review the uses of public land and call into question those, like the still-popular tradition of hunting with dogs, that might injure cougars. Officials of all kinds would also have to undertake an educational campaign to teach people how to live with an animal that can, and occasionally does, eat humans.

Shyness is the norm for cougars, but historical records show them quite capable of treating people, especially children, as prey. There's at least one tombstone in the East, dated 1751 in Chester County, Pennsylvania, that marks a settler's death by cougar. Native Americans must surely have now and then lost some wide-roaming children. Today, cougar attacks have increased dramatically out West, as human sprawl crowds into cougar country. More people—a total of nine—have been killed by cougars in the twenty-five years from 1973 to 1998 than in all of the previous century. I feel no fear, though, as I pad along the moss-carpeted old logging roads that now serve as forest paths. I almost wish I did.

The once-gashed roads I follow are part of the legacy of irony that I have inherited in Appalachia, my chosen home. It was the destruction of Appalachia's fabulous hardwood forests by private loggers that prompted the government to buy up seven million acres of national forest and parklands for restoration. Stretching down the southern Appalachian Mountains from Virginia to Alabama, these now comprise the largest complex of federal lands east of the Mississippi. Here lies the eastern cougar's best hope for the future. My property borders the George Washington National Forest, at the northern threshold of that geography of hope. If cougars are making it anywhere in the East, sooner or later they ought to be in my backyard.

My yard is an open half-acre of meadow and garden, a tiny tear in the forest that sweeps down Cross Mountain over my shoulders like a cloak. By counting tree rings as we cut firewood, my husband and I have found that most of our trees are between eighty and ninety years old. By this, by the U.S. Forest Service archives for the area, and by an iron-wheeled lumbering crane rusting on a nearby ridge, we can date the last major cutting cycle through our woods to around 1910–20. This was the height of the great Appalachian lumber boom. Floods became common as whole mountainsides were denuded and left exposed to erosion. Limbs left by loggers dried out, were ignited by sparks from steam-powered trains and sawmills, and fueled wildfire after withering wildfire. On many of my acres I find old fire-charred stumps, one of them twenty feet high and deeply blackened to the top. It terrifies me to imagine those moments when that tree was burning.

By then, white-tailed deer, the favorite prey of cougars, had already been hunted to the point that merely seeing a set of tracks made for a local event. Unable to recover on their own, deer were restocked on national forest lands in most Appalachian states. They have since prospered only too well. Farmers and foresters alike complain about heavy browsing by deer. Lyme disease, spread by a type of deer tick, has become locally common in recent years. We've learned not to plant certain ornamentals because the deer invariably eat them. A doe took residence near the house several years ago, and periodically I stumble onto a spotted fawn in a brushy patch. The forest, too, has recovered, though it is only a ghost of its former self, and has lost so much topsoil it can never reclaim its former glory. There are a few white oaks on my land now that are just a little bigger than my arms can encircle. Good habitat and abundant prey are once again available. Most biologists agree that human attitudes are the only limiting factor for eastern cougars.

The psychology of cougar sightings is convoluted. People who think they've seen a cougar resist the obvious and logical explanations. "It was a dog," I told Lori, Willy, Gil, and Dave, only to be met with angry stares. They want to believe they've seen the rarest and most dangerous animal possible where they live. Surely these cougars are cultural projections, drawn perhaps from guilt for our collective ravaging of the continent, or from yearning for the exoneration that the survival of cougars would confer. Surely, too, there is an element of thrill-seeking in the sightings, in a culture addicted to the fastest, highest, and fiercest, whether in machines, mountains, or animals. Maybe the image of cat goes deeper than culture. Maybe it has been permanently etched on human consciousness by eons of that peculiar tension between fear and admiration, the anxiety of ambivalence. Cat sightings may be a primal expression of the human understanding of nature. I peer at whiskery arrangements of twigs and leaves in the shadowy undergrowth of my forest, and my back awaits the sensation of cat eyes on it.

Despite the chaos of cultural images, in the burgeoning mass of eastern cougar sightings there is a small core of utterly convincing accounts. Respected naturalists have reported encounters with cougars. People with no woods experience have noted details of cougar appearance and behavior that they could not have known. I have myself seen a home video filmed in western Maryland in 1992 that showed an unmistakable cougar stepping momentarily between trees in a forest. The 1990s brought much more proof of cougar existence than any agency wants to admit. The Canadian province of New Brunswick confirmed cougar presence there in 1993 by analyzing a scat collected by a provincial biologist. It had cougar hairs in it, presumed to be ingested during self-grooming. A year or two later, Maine state biologists verified cougar tracks. The U.S. Fish and Wildlife Service confirmed three cougars—a mother with young—in Vermont in 1994, by the same kind of analysis done in New Brunswick. In

1997, Shenandoah National Park was swamped with so many credible cougar sightings that park biologists set up baited camera stations, hoping (in vain as yet) to get a picture. The next year, a committee of the Virginia legislature agreed to recompense a mountain farmer in southwest Virginia whose pygmy goats were believed killed by a cougar. The farmer sought repayment from the state because cougars are protected by the Endangered Species Act and he couldn't go after the one he blamed for killing his livestock. At the same time, state biologists in Tennessee were rubbing their chins over some plaster track casts they had taken near the Cumberland Plateau, on the western edge of Appalachia.

So much persuasive evidence has accumulated that the wildlife establishment is beginning to acknowledge it, sort of. Instead of denying all possibilities of cougar existence, officials are routinely quoted as saying that yes, there may be a few cougars out there, but they're all escaped or released captives that originated in the western U.S. or South America, not remnant natives. (Even the thirty to fifty remaining Florida panthers, the only officially acknowledged population of eastern cougars, were castigated by opponents of the recovery program when it was learned that some Florida panthers had an ancestor from South America.) Therefore, these cats being seen in the East aren't really eastern cougars at all. By implication, they aren't entitled to the protections of the Endangered Species Act. It's a handy way to sidestep any responsibility for a wide-ranging, threatening predator.

And there's likely a large grain of truth in the claim that at least some eastern cougars are former pets. There's an astounding market, legal and illegal, in exotic felines. I've read ads in newspapers and magazines for cougar kittens, and out of curiosity once wrote for a price list from an animal farm in South Carolina. Cougar kittens were on sale at the time for $850. Adults were cheaper at $600, and jaguars, leopards, black leopards, Bengal tigers, and something called a "leopard jaguar" were available upon request (and—this was noted in small print—with the proper Department of Interior permits) for $1,250 to $2,000. Federal laws are a maze, states have varying or no regulations, and estimates are virtually impossible, but where exotic cats can be reckoned, they number in the thousands. Talk about the human psychology of cats! Not to mention the rationalizing needed to justify caging a large animal designed by two million years of evolution to run free.

Endearingly cute as kittens, cougars grow into unpredictable, voracious adults. Surely, some number of fearful or exasperated owners have driven to the nearest forested area and opened the gate. The survival chances of such human-raised cougars are unclear. Lacking instruction from a mother, would their hunting ability be adequate? Some biologists with experience in cougar adaptability think so. The abundance of small prey in the eastern woods, including raccoons, opossums, skunks, and ground nesting birds, might just supply enough food until a cougar taught him- or herself how to bring down deer. How much would being declawed hinder them? Not long ago I asked the owner of two pet cougars, who come at her call and lick her hands, how many captive cats are declawed. She is involved in various wild cat associations and knows many owners, and said she thought quite a few, if not most of them, declawed their pets. The expert I consulted on cougar biology would say only that declawing would certainly be a disadvantage, but beyond that nothing was known.

So in addition to any last lone eastern natives that might have survived the timbering holocaust, captive-raised cats from other cougar populations are probably loose out there. To these two sources might be added a third: the migration of cougars out of the west, northeast around the Great Lakes, and down the Appalachian spine. Coyotes did it; why not cougars? There are fragments of evidence to support such speculation, like cougars being documented in recent years in Canada in places where they have never been seen before. Throughout the East, the number of credible accounts of a mother with young point toward reproduction. My own theory is that at this moment in time, as the millennium turns, we have a proto-population of eastern cougars composed of mongrels.

I say "proto" because studies done as part of the Florida panther recovery program showed that a very small cougar population can be very fluid, its social network too weak to hold individual members firmly in place over time. Individuals wandered all around, rather than staying in one home range. In larger populations, home territories tend to be more defined, with the best habitats kept constantly tenanted. In those places, evidence of cougar presence is easily found. Where cougars are far fewer and more transient, their sign will naturally be rare. And they will likely wander until they meet their fate or a mate, whichever comes first. It remains to be seen if eastern cougars, from whatever source, can multiply enough to bind themselves in place and, finally, to fully reveal themselves.

I call them "mongrels" for a reason as well. Biologists are just as vulnerable to racism as anyone else, and a demand for racial "purity" can corrupt science just as surely as it does human relations. By its own tools, science has now proved that purity is nothing more than a human concept, with little application in the wild. For four years, I tracked a doctoral student working on a dissertation to analyze DNA from all subspecies of cougar. To represent eastern cougars, which were almost exterminated before anyone thought to keep museum specimens, the student collected tissue from six pelts. The conclusion: that the fifteen subspecies of North American cougars had too little genetic variation to warrant subspecies classification, and should be reduced to one. Taxonomists have been too eager to freeze dynamic interactions into static categories. There is simply no way, based on the handful of specimens available, to positively define an eastern cougar as uniquely distinct from other cougars. It doesn't make a whit of difference where those cougars in the eastern woods come from. They are all capable of filling the eastern cougar niche. We ought to be grateful to them for their courage in trying.

A Cherokee lady I recently met asked me if I ever felt a cougar in my woods. I had to say I didn't. I want to, because I long for the benediction that the sight of a cougar might bring, but I know desire can deceive. I rein my mind in from its probing through the forest, and try to put cat images aside. Yet there is an image that haunts me, not only when I am in the woods. It comes from the true story of the cougars of Paddy Mountain, a few miles north of my house. In the snowy winter of 1850, local farmers tracked two of the last cougars in Virginia along the crest of Paddy Mountain, where boulders stand tall and flat-faced as houses. One cat, the male sibling of the pair, was shot, and someone from the Smithsonian Institution collected his skeleton the following spring. One hundred and forty-three years later, in a small room equipped for the preparation of specimens, I held the poor shattered bones of that male cougar in my hands. His sister escaped. I see her crouched in a rock den on Paddy Mountain, high above the valley, her muscles taut. I see her yellow eyes gleaming in the dimness of the cave. She does not look at me, but beyond, maybe into the future.

A Multitude
of Witnesses

by Barbara Dean

In the late spring of 1995, as required by California law, we—the joint partnership of which I am one member—were notified that the steep, mixed conifer- and hardwood-covered hillside to the west of our land was scheduled for logging. This would be the fourth "timber harvest" on those slopes in the twenty-five years since my thirteen co-owners and I bought our square mile of rugged, isolated land in the Coast Range of northern California. Until the notification, we hadn't known that Louisiana-Pacific Corporation, our original neighbor, had sold the property. The new owner is a private corporation I've never heard of, whose central offices are located on the coast, three hours away.

The property to be logged is the hillside from which our drinking water comes; streams formed by natural springs and rainfall are gathered by the folds of the hill and pulled by gravity, then partly diverted into our homes and holding tanks on their way to the river below. This is also the hillside—hidden by mist on winter mornings, glowing with soft color in the fall and translucent new growth in the spring—that I gaze at each day when Koba, my Rhodesian Ridgeback puppy, and I cross our seven-acre meadow to check the mailbox on the county road. My western horizon is this familiar, jagged, fir-pierced skyline, behind which the sun sets each evening. Because of the way the land fits together, someone standing under those trees can hear the voices of people walking in our meadow. Black-tailed deer, black bears, brown bats, red-tailed hawks, mountain lions, dragonflies, rattlesnakes, spotted skunks—most of the creatures who share these hills—move across the boundaries without noticing. In every sense except the one that suddenly matters, our land and the land to be logged seem of a piece.

When we bought this land in 1971, that hillside was virgin forest. One summer afternoon in those early years, I hiked past our property line to the top of the ridge, scrambling up the steep grade in dappled sunlight, under towering Douglas firs and yellow pines so big I couldn't begin to encircle them with my arms. I particularly remember the smell of deep, dark soil, pungent even in the heat of summer, and the muted calls of birds and squirrels, sounds cushioned by rich humus and foliage. This forest was a world apart from the logged-over slopes of our ranch.

In the mid-1970s, when Louisiana-Pacific decided to cut their trees for the first time, we set out to convince the California Department of Forestry that this was exactly the kind of land that should never be logged. Even then, naive as we were, we understood that an emotional plea to preserve a virgin hillside was unlikely to prevail. Instead we argued in terms of economic and human self-interest that this hillside was too steep to cut economically, safely, and sustainably, that its soil was too vulnerable to erosion, and that the water quality of its streams was too important to jeopardize.

Needless to say, we weren't successful. During the first severe winter after the logging, we watched our fears become fact: the earthen dam that served as holding tank for our main water system silted in completely, since the uphill trees whose roots had kept the soil in place until then were no longer there.

Twenty years later, our goals are more realistic—we have no illusions of halting the cut, but we want to minimize the damage to our water. The property to be logged is 274 acres of mixed coniferous forest, with some slopes exceeding 65 percent. We have five developed springs within 1000 feet of the boundary. I have recently set up a small hydropower generator that provides winter electricity to my home office, where I work full-time (I am an editor for a publisher of environmental books). The hydro is situated near the creek below my house, so in addition to worries about gritty or polluted drinking and bathing water, I fear that too much silt and debris in the water may clog the pipes and damage the alternator—effectively paralyzing my office during the months when there isn't enough sun to supply my solar panels.

———

The logging equipment rolls down the country road in early October, and the sound of backhoes and Caterpillars repairing old logging trails echoes through the mountain air. On the first day of the cut, a Saturday in mid-October, Koba and I walk through the meadow at noon to get the mail. The sun is high in the sky, and the hills are resplendent with color. The deep green of the conifers and live oaks contrasts with the red of poison oak, the bright yellow of an occasional maple, and the tans of the deciduous oaks, just beginning to turn.

From our meadow, I can hear the chain saws, but I can't quite see them. I search the hillside, trying to locate the loggers. And then my eye catches movement—and I watch a majestic

Douglas fir begin to topple in slow motion. Koba startles as the sound of the initial crack reaches us out of sync a second later, and then we hear the tree creak and groan (I try not to think of it as screaming, but . . .) as it falls to earth. The tree bounces, a dust cloud rises. Finally there is only a black hole where the big tree had been—and silence, except for the pounding of my heart.

Since we have been through this before, I know what to expect from now until the end of logging season. Pre-dawn to dusk noise: chain saws, huge trucks, Caterpillars; the bells of big equipment backing up, the sounds of loggers shouting to each other. From within my house, the sounds are dampened, but as soon as I step outside, the noise drops on me like an unwelcome cloak. I face the weeks ahead with resignation, grateful for the demands of my job, which force my attention away from the logging most of the time. I am determined not to get emotionally involved; having agonized over previous "harvests," I know that getting upset disrupts my own life but not the logging.

Weeks pass; the cutting continues. Despite my efforts to shield myself from the logging activity and focus instead on the work on my desk, by late November, after I snap at three different authors in one day, I have to acknowledge how tense I have become. My stomach is knotted with anxiety—and has been, now that I think of it, for a long time. I am already planning a short trip to visit friends on the coming weekend; now I realize how badly I need the break.

By Friday afternoon, I am looking forward to getting away from the chain saws, but am also nervous about leaving the ranch unoccupied for two days (the ranch caretaker will be gone, too) with a logging crew composed of strangers so close. Late in the day, while I am behind my house preparing the car for the trip, I hear a rasping cry that sounds like my cat, Deacon. Since I know Deacon is in the house, I assume I am hearing the stray kitten I had glimpsed earlier in the week. But when I look up, expecting to see the small gray body, it seems that nothing is there.

I return to the house, where Koba is standing on her toes at the front door, quivering with intensity, barking ferociously. Ridgebacks are not big barkers, so I always take notice when Koba decides that something is worthy of that kind of attention. Even though I am pretty sure that she must just be reacting to the stray cat, who probably scampered around to the front of the house, I go to the door and follow Koba's gaze.

And when I look, instead of a small gray kitty, I see the long, powerful, tawny body of a mountain lion, loping across the meadow less than twenty feet from my door. This is the biggest lion I have seen in twenty-five years here; he (or she) stretches six feet or more from nose to haunch, followed by another three feet of formidable, sweeping tail. Muscles rippling, eyes straight ahead, the lion appears strong, healthy, and *angry*: I can hear him complaining—yowling and scolding—and see his tail lashing as it whips the air. He looks and sounds just like an angry house-cat—a *large* angry housecat. With my skin tingling, I realize that this is the same sound I heard behind the house. Where was the lion when I was packing the car?

I have never seen Koba so excited. Hackles straight up, tail extended, head stretched high, her entire young being is focused on the lion. Ridgebacks were originally bred in Africa to track lions and keep them at bay until the hunters arrived. All those African instincts seem to have been triggered by the sight of this continent's big cat. Koba's barking chops and roils the air like a boulder dropped into a mountain pool. The lion must be able to hear the noise through the windows and walls of the house; however, he doesn't even glance toward us.

Like Koba, I am transfixed. But it is some measure of how distanced I have become from the natural life around me that while part of my mind is drinking in the cat's lovely, fluid form and watching him with awe, another part is thinking, "Omigod, I'm not going to be able to take a walk without worrying about being attacked." Images of joggers being jumped by lions race through my mind, followed by statistics from a conference session I attended last summer about the increasing mountain lion–human interactions in California. I remember that forty miles from the ranch, a rabid lion bit several people and a dog around a campfire one night last spring; a few months earlier, in the foothills of the Sierras, a female jogger was killed and eaten.

When the lion passes into the woods and out of sight, I open the door. Koba races to the front fence, and I walk to the edge of the porch, which changes my perspective considerably. No longer is my view restricted by window frames, my senses of smell and hearing disrupted by window glass and wood siding, my place on the hillside circumscribed by brick walls and beam ceiling. Now I am in a part of the meadow; I can smell the traces of camphor in the late season grasses, feel the autumn sky overhead.

The lion's complaining voice is still clear as he descends the hill toward the creek. But in my mind the media images of mountain lion attacks fade, replaced by memories of the other living lions I have seen on this hillside. The first, who didn't appear until I had lived here for fifteen years, and then strolled behind my house one Sunday morning just a few weeks after I had dreamed of a lion giving birth. The mother and three adolescents, who leaped and soared across the meadow below the house a few years later, lifting my spirits when I was distraught about the impending death of Nandi, my last Ridgeback, Koba's predecessor. The pair of young lions, probably siblings, whom I watched for forty-five minutes one summer evening in this same meadow as they tried to hunt, with me aware each second how extraordinary it was to be able to watch this event, commonplace for the lions but very rarely seen by humans.

A handful of encounters in twenty-five years, each one unique and compelling. Each lingered for weeks and months in my psyche. Even now, the memories quicken my heartbeat.

Although the late afternoon sun still lights the meadow, my place on the porch is in shadow. I can hear the cat yowling and scolding, still apparently furious, as he crosses the creek and climbs the hill in front of me. At the same time, behind me, I am suddenly aware of the whine of chain saws and grinding of machinery.

And just as suddenly, the emotion I have tried to suppress for weeks erupts within me. I think of the mountain lion habitat up and down the state that is being "developed" into housing sub-divisions or converted to farmland, and I wonder if this cat has just discovered Caterpillar tractors destroying a favorite haunt up the hill. Of course it's impossible for me to know why the lion is so upset. But at this moment, I have no doubt that he's com-plaining about what is happening on that hillside. In this moment, this beautiful, powerful, *angry* animal embodies all my emotion and pain, expressing exactly what I want to say to the loggers: "Get out of here, damn it, with your noise and greed! Leave this place wild and in peace!"

———

It's not until months later, midwinter, when the chain saws are finally silent, that I have some quiet time to reflect on the events of the summer and fall, and to tease apart the connections among the logging, the mountain lion, and my own psyche. In the dark-ness of winter, with the soil and remaining trees on that hillside more exposed to winter storms, the creeks swollen with rain, I contemplate my initial fearful response to the big cat.

In twenty-five years of living in near-wilderness, I have learned that there are many different kinds of fear and, gener-ally, that fear brings me closer to the natural world. For example, fear sharpens my senses when the rattlesnakes have emerged from winter sleep and I am walking around the land, with my eyes alert for a snake's movement or pattern and ears cocked for the telltale slither. I feel a tingling nervousness when I come across a fresh pile of black bear droppings—and quickly look over my shoulder.

After each of my previous encounters with mountain lions, I took a distinctly heightened sense of caution into the woods, my perceptions suddenly alert to the possibility of another pair of eyes lurking among the trees. But the flash of fear I felt when I saw this big cat, instead of tying me into the landscape, made me want to shut myself off from the world around me.

As I thought about what was different this time, my mind kept returning to the logging. The noise and overwhelming presence of the timber harvest had filled my waking hours and even my dreams during most of the fall. I had consciously tried to keep some emotional distance from what was happening on that hillside, to avoid the feelings that welled up naturally within. But now I wondered about the cost of that strategy.

—

Over the months, as I pondered the consequences to our psyches, both individual and collective, of ignoring our innate emotional and spiritual connections with the natural world, one image repeatedly pushed into my mind: the picture of Koba facing her first mountain lion.

Although Ridgebacks were bred in Africa to help with hunting lions, Koba herself, at eighteen months, had never seen a lion—nor, certainly, had her parents or grandparents. Koba was a cautious pup, and before the event, if I'd tried to guess how she would respond to an angry lion, I probably would have recalled her first encounter with fresh bear scent. One summer day when she was only four months old and we were walking through the meadow, Koba paused, sniffed the dusty path and then the afternoon breeze, looked around quickly, and sat down, flatly refusing to follow me. At the time, since I couldn't smell the bear, her behavior puzzled me; it wasn't until a neighbor told me he had seen a bear in that precise spot an hour before that I understood.

But something about this lion—the shape and movement of the lion's muscular body, perhaps his savanna-like color and flowing tail, or maybe his guttural cries—must have touched a genetic memory and aroused the hunter latent within. In response, every muscle in Koba's own tawny body quivered;

every daunting bit of canine attention focused on that big cat. She wanted to *go after that lion.* I could almost hear her thinking, "Aha! So *this* is what life is all about!"

Watching Koba, whose presence in my life invigorates my own animal senses, felt like beholding the deep rush and engagement of instinct: that complex and ineffable link between inner and outer, between the animal and her environment. The lion stretched and redefined Koba's sense of identity, and challenged her to possibilities that until then she hadn't even known existed.

We don't call it "instinct" in humans, but the multifaceted, visceral connections between our species and the natural world are just as profound—and, in my experience, are a source of equal power and promise. Just as surely as the lion is part of Koba's genetic memory, so is an enveloping wild landscape teeming with other creatures central to our original understanding of the world and our rightful place within it. This original sense of "home" illuminates the rest of my story of the day the mountain lion appeared.

I had been packing to leave for the weekend and was nervous about leaving the ranch alone. I was emotionally drained from the burden of watching over the land, protecting it not specifically from any direct action by the loggers but just from the sense of looming danger and imminent destruction that had saturated the atmosphere for weeks. I could feel the tension in my body; the muscles in my shoulders were taut and aching.

And then this beautiful, wild, angry carnivore appeared—an unexpected visitor whose presence expressed and reflected all the anger and violence and grief on the hillside, including my own. With the big cat's cries fading across the creek, his commanding image still hovering in the meadow, I lingered on the porch, savoring the cat's graceful form, the rasp of his voice, wanting to hold the memory of his appearance and make it part of me.

When I finally turned to finish packing, I realized that the muscles in my shoulders had relaxed. Although my worries hadn't disappeared, I no longer felt alone in my angst. The lion not only seemed to share my pain and anger but also by his very "otherness" welcomed me back into the company of life on the hillside.

The vague loneliness that had been with me all fall, since the cutting started, since I tried to withdraw my attention from the forest, dissolved. Deep within, I felt restored to the natural life around me, reconnected to the black-tailed doe who comes out of the trees at sunrise and the turkey vultures who soar overhead in the late afternoon and the madrone tree patiently waiting for another spring. My spirit was fortified by the presence of all these other lives who were here before the loggers arrived, as I was, and who will be here after the loggers leave, as I will be.

Linked by our changed hillside, this diverse community of life will greet the winter rains, which will wash away too much soil under the trees that no longer live on the steep slopes. And in the spring, when the madrone glows with new flowers, manzanita and ceanothus bushes will sprout where some of the big trees used to grow. Who knows if the lion will pass this way again, or if he will notice the black bear who will lumber across the rocky bank, avoiding the men who will return to take the last of the trees?

When darkness finally takes over the hills, Koba climbs into the car. As happens each time I turn down the winding dirt road toward town, I feel my love for this place course through my blood and muscles, pulling at my heart. Tonight, I reach out to touch Koba's warm body in the seat next to mine. She glances at me briefly, then perks her ears and focuses her attention on the road ahead. I, too, look forward, and step a little harder on the gas, my emotions full, knowing that these hills we love are attended by a multitude of witnesses.

Lion Eyes

by Terry Tempest Williams

It was going to be a long ride home for fifteen Navajo children. Dropping kids off five, ten, and twenty miles apart is no small task. We were committed for the night. The sun had just vanished behind Giant's Knuckles, causing those in the back of the pickup to huddle close.

"It gets cold in the desert," I said.

"It's winter," one of the children replied. They covered their mouths with their hands, giggling, as we continued to bump along the dirt roads surrounding Montezuma Creek. What did the driver and I know? We were Anglos.

We had been down by the river for the afternoon. A thin

veneer of ice had coalesced along its edge, and the children, bending down, would break off pieces and hold them between their thumbs and forefingers. Before the ice would melt, some brought the thin sheet to their eyes as a lens, while others placed it on their mouths and sucked on the river. Still others winged the ice sheets across the cobbles, watching, listening to them shatter like glass.

Life on the river's edge was explored through whirligig beetles, water skaters, and caddis fly larvae under stones. Canada geese flew above the channel, landing for brief intervals, then continuing on their way. The children followed tracks, expecting to meet a pack of stray dogs hiding in the tamarisks. Our shadows grew longer with the last light of day reflecting on river rapids and willows.

The hours by the river were all spent. Now, in the back of the pickup, the children told tales of days when a horse could enter a hogan and leave as a man; of skinwalkers disguised as coyotes who stalk the reservation with bones in their hands, scratching white crosses on the doors of ill-fated households. They spoke of white owls, ghostly flashes of light that could turn the blood of mice into milk.

Just then, my friend hit the brakes and those of us in the back fell forward.

"What was that?" The driver leaned his head out the window so we could hear him. "Did you see that?"

"What?" we all asked.

"A mountain lion! It streaked across the road. I'll swear it was all tail!"

The children whispered among themselves, "Mountain Lion . . ."

We filed out of the truck. My friend and I walked a few feet ahead. We found the tracks. A rosette. Four-toed pads, clawless, imprinted on the sand in spite of the cold.

"No question," I said. "Lion. I wonder where she is now?"

Looking into the darkness, I could only imagine the desert

cat staring back at us. I looked over at the children; most of them were leaning against the truck as headlights approached.

"What's going on?" a local Navajo asked as he rolled down the window of his pickup with his motor idling.

My friend recognized him as the uncle of one of the children. "We think we saw a mountain lion," he said.

"Where? How long ago?"

The other man in the cab of the truck asked if we were sure.

"Pretty sure," I said. "Look at these tracks."

The men got out of their vehicles and shined their flashlights on the ground until they picked up the prints. One of the men knelt down and touched them.

"This is not good," the uncle said. "They will kill our sheep." He looked into the night and then back at us. "What color of eyes did it have?"

My friend and I looked at each other. The Navajo elder began reciting the color of animals' eyes at night.

"Deer's eyes are blue. Coyote's eyes are red." His nephew interrupted him. "Green—the lion's eyes were green."

The two men said they would be back with their guns and sons tomorrow.

We returned to the truck, the driver with a handful of kids up front and the rest in back around me as we nestled together under blankets. The children became unusually quiet, speaking in low, serious voices about why mountain lions are considered dangerous.

"It's more than just killing sheep," one child explained. "Mountain Lion is a god, one of the supernaturals that has power over us."

Each child gave away little bits of knowledge concerning the lion: that it chirps like a bird to fool you; that parts of its body are used for medicine; that in the old days, hunters used the sinew of the lion for their bows. The children grew more and more anxious as fear seized their voices like two hands around their throats. They were hushed.

We traveled through the starlit desert in silence, except for the hum of the motor and four wheels flying over the washboard.

In time, from the rear of the pickup, came a slow deliberate chant. Navajo words—gentle, deep meanderings of music born out of healing. I could not tell who had initiated the song, but one by one each child entered the melody. Over and over they sang the same monotonous notes, dreamlike at first, until gradually the cadence quickened. The children's mood began to lighten, and they swayed back and forth. What had begun as a cautious, fearful tone emerged as a joyous one. Their elders had taught them well. They had sung themselves back to *hózhó*, where the world is balanced and whole.

After the last child had been taken home, my friend and I were left with each other, but the echo of the children's chant remained. With many miles to go, we rolled down the windows in the cab of the truck, letting the chilled air blow through. Mountain Lion, whose eyes I did not see, lay on the mesa, her whiskers retrieving each note carried by the wind.

Looking for
Abbey's Lion

by Pam Houston

Eleven years ago, when I was a senior in college in Ohio, when the farthest west I had been was across the Indiana border one drunken night when a boyfriend and I drove to my mother's hometown and stole the Lion's Club's WELCOME TO SPICELAND, INDIANA sign, a good friend introduced me to the works of Edward Abbey. I devoured *Desert Solitaire* first, then *The Journey Home, Down the River, Beyond the Wall, Black Sun,* and *The Monkey Wrench Gang.* Abbey lived in the heart of wild country I could scarcely imagine as I looked out over those low green Midwestern hills: jagged granite peaks, silver in the twilight, bright orange labyrinths of twisted sandstone, wide rivers of thick muddy water moving through canyon walls five times higher than the tallest hill I could see from my dorm. The fact that Abbey was, like me, from a small town in Pennsylvania seemed rife with significance. If he could claim the West as his latter-day home, perhaps one day I could too.

Of all the writing by Abbey that stays in my accessible memory, my favorite passage is one that appears in *The Journey Home* in an essay titled "Freedom and Wilderness, Wilderness and Freedom." Abbey is doing his usual canyon hike: too long, no water, too close to dark. He's found some mountain lion tracks halfway up the canyon, and since he's never seen a mountain lion, he's decided to follow them. But night comes down on him quickly, and he's forced to give up the search and turn around. As he walks through the gathering darkness toward the mouth of the canyon, he hears footsteps behind him, once, twice, three times. They seem to stop when he stops, begin again when he walks on. Fear mounting inside of him, he swivels suddenly, sharp and fast, and sees the lion, only fifty yards behind him, massive in the twilight and sleek, one paw raised in the air as if in greeting, yellow eyes unblinking and cool. Abbey holds out his own hand and takes three slow steps toward the cat before he comes to his senses and decides he's not quite ready to shake a mountain lion's paw. The lion watches Abbey descend toward what's left of the light at the bottom of the canyon, unmoving, paw still raised.

The magic of that passage for me is contained in the moment of decision, the tension between Abbey's wanting to embrace that lion as if they were friends who'd met up after many years' separation, and his eventual respect for the lion's wildness, his recognition of the distance that must be maintained between the wild thing and himself, his understanding that wanting to shake the lion's paw must, for the time being, be enough.

I read that essay eleven years ago not knowing, in any exact sense, what a mountain lion looked like, not knowing, for that matter, what a canyon hike was. The one thing I did know, even then, is that I wanted to feel the spark of raw, communicable energy that translated between man and beast in Abbey's story, and that if I could ever stand face to face for even one brief moment with a mountain lion I would have learned something invaluable about my life.

I headed west for the first time at the end of my senior year, and from the Missouri border on I kept my eyes trained on the sagebrush-sided highways, on the dense rocky outcroppings, hoping for a glimpse of Abbey's lion. And that first, awe-filled summer, when it seemed I couldn't keep my eyes open wide enough, long enough, to take the big country in, when it seemed I couldn't listen hard enough, breathe fast enough, walk far enough to do the land any kind of justice, I added hike after hike to my new life's list of accomplishments, my eyes always ready for a flash of feline muscle, my ears straining for the soft fall of padded feet. I sighted fresh tracks once, and older ones maybe half a dozen times, but I never rounded the corner in time to see the tip of a tail disappearing, and no yellow eyes ever turned around to follow me back down-canyon, and no muscley beast ever raised his paw in salute to me.

The West captured my soul and imagination like nothing before in my life. I cut my ties to the East and moved west permanently, my jobs cycling through the seasons, changing always in the direction of less and less pay per hour, and more and more hours outside. From a bartender to a bus driver to a highway flagger to a park ranger paid only as a volunteer, I finally settled into a career as a river and wilderness guide, my hours outside outnumbering those inside by almost four to one.

In eleven years of hiking, boating, guiding, and exploring, I've come face to face with nearly every North American game species. I've watched a female black bear and her cubs gorge themselves on huckleberries, heard a big bull elk bugling not ten feet from my ear. I've had a timber wolf walk right through my campsite as if he intended to join me for dinner, and I've had an abandoned mule deer fawn come and eat grass out of my hand. I've walked through thick pine trees right into the knees of a confused cow moose, opened my eyes in the middle of the night to the inquisitive sniffing of a porcupine, watched a group of bighorn lambs play a very complicated game of King of the Hill on a craggy peak not twenty yards away. I've seen the hot puffy breath of a bison break the clarity of a frozen Yellowstone morning, and the first white fur of winter appear on the considerable feet of a snowshoe hare. I've followed a single coyote for miles across slickrock in hazy moonlight, and walked among a herd of pronghorn in the still heat of a high desert day. I've watched lynx, bobcat, ptarmigan, rattlesnake, golden eagles, white tails, javelinas, and hawks, and stumbled across more big male grizzly bears than any one person ought to be allowed and still be around to tell about it. But I've still never come face to face with Abbey's lion.

It is clear to me, only now, that I came to live in the West not because I would see a mountain lion, but because I might see one. (If what I really wanted was to see a mountain lion, I could have lived down the street from the Bronx Zoo.) And though I couldn't have imagined it from my dorm room in Ohio, the mountain lion has taught me his lesson not through a face-to-face encounter but through his elusiveness and intangibility. The mountain lion's lesson for me has been one of patience; even more correctly, it has been a lesson in the value of uncaptured dreams. For as much as I have loved the heart-stopping surprise of my encounters with bear, with wolf, with coyote, they cannot match the power and purity of my unrequited desire to see Abbey's lion. A dream unrealized, the lion has taught me, is the essential food of the soul.

And I have imagined him, so many times, the way he will stand, his fur, shades of dusky gold in the late afternoon sunlight, his eyes suggesting a game I'll most likely not play. He is with me always, this lion of my imagination. He will keep my eyes wide open as I'm walking through the canyons. He will keep my love and wonder at the landscape that surrounds me ever rare, ever young.

Wildcats I Have Not Known

by Annick Smith

They are near to me. I have seen their tracks in the mud of logging roads and in the snow on Bear Creek's bottoms. The tracks
are rounded. Four-toed. With no claw marks because the lion's
claws are retracted when she walks. Her footprints are larger
than those of the huge yellow dog who lives down the road, but
unlike a dog she walks a straight line. Or nearly straight. The
line of a stalker.

I have walked the trails the wildcats walk for nearly thirty
years, yet I have never learned to think like a cat. My tracks are
splayed, meandering. Some days I walk with my sons, or my
true companion, or friends, but usually I walk alone and always

with dogs—the German shepherds I understand—Sylvie, black and tan, who came to the ranch when our kids were young; Rasta, alpha-bright and golden; her daughter Betty, my placid pal these grandmother days. I have walked with our black Lab, Shy Moon, and my dear, lost Little Red Dog, but I have never laid eyes on a mountain lion, not even one of the bobcats who also reside in these Montana foothills.

Maybe it's the dogs who scare them off—the old enmities— but I doubt if a mountain lion is so easily scared. The cat, as Rudyard Kipling noted, walks by itself and, when it chooses, remains invisible. Perhaps that flash of amber up in the shadowy branches of a yellow pine is a wildcat's dark-tipped switchy tail. Or he's hiding under slabs of lichen-green rock on the cliff where I stand looking down at my meadow. I feel uneasy, vulnerable. I turn from the dark woods and head for home.

A scream in the night lifts the hair on my neck. It could be the scream of a fawn in the lion's jaws, or it could be the lion's mating cry—life and death so connected I cannot distinguish one from the other. Fearful, I call in my three housecats. Looking into the cloud-black sky, no stars or moon or yellow lights of houses, I am surrounded by presences I love and cannot see, including the ghost cats who are my neighbors, and I am fully alive. The wildcats make me happy because as long as they inhabit my world, I know it is, at least in this way, wild.

———

I live in the midst of a meadow that spills from pine-timbered ridges along a creek called Bear, for obvious reasons, into the valley of the Big Blackfoot River a mile or so to the north. It is a cupped opening hacked out of the virgin forest more than a century ago by immigrant Swedes. My circle of grass is domesticated, like grazing horses and cattle and me. Outside its margins lie miles of unpeopled country, which though roaded and scarred by logging is still the domain of wild animals.

I sit in my hewn-log house and look out tall windows across

open ground to a ragged, latticed line of firs, ponderosas, and western larch. The edge of meadow and forest is clear as a wall, but unlike a wall it is open. On my round oak table are binoculars through which I observe the beings who bridge the gap from trees to grass.

Whitetail deer emerge in early morning light. Compared to the heavy-bodied cows, they are delicate, pale, evanescent. Summer nights I catch their yellow eyes in my headlights. The deer have descended on my garden to munch the lettuce, browse my petunias. Lazy Betty doesn't even bark. I honk my horn. The deer bound over the fence into the meadow and all I can see is the white gleam of their upraised flags.

Often I hear coyotes yapping. They have become bold because they know it is safe here. They play catch-me-if-you-can with my dog, pounce on gophers who burrow in rockpiles. Elk appear at dusk in May, high-stepping out of the pines in search of pink-centered flowers called spring beauties. The leader arches her neck like a camel, snout up to catch any scent of danger. Yearlings buck and chase. When night falls, some will bed on the meadow. I will see the imprint of their bodies tomorrow in the bent grass.

In autumn, when tart wild apples hang red from the volunteer tree by my woodshed and the thornapple brush is heavy with berries, we may be lucky at dawn to spot an elusive black bear, perhaps with cubs. We used to see so many bears that we named a hollow in our woods Bear Cove. But they have been hunted and hounded and now I see only the steaming piles of berry-rich scat. I am content with that, satisfied the bears are still in the neighborhood.

My blood runs fast at the spectacle of wild creatures on my meadow or in the woods where I walk. I have been known to get teary at the sight of a traveling moose, a great horned owl, the bluebirds and kestrels who return with the runoff in March. Songs of spring peepers, the whirring whistle of snipe diving from the sky in their mating ritual, a drumbeat thrum of grouse, the red-tailed hawk who screeches as I pass his snag bring a kind of ecstasy, but I am still waiting for my mountain lion, my lynx and bobcats. Others have spotted them.

———

Once we had chickens. White leghorns arrived in a box as downy chicks, ordered from a catalog. My husband, Dave, had grown up in rural Minnesota and loved to wake to the cock's alarm, and so we ordered a dozen hens and a dozen roosters. Big mistake. The roosters formed a gang. They would follow my four-year-old twins, attacking from the rear. The older boys armed the twins with bricks and taught them to use a rusted frying pan to beat off the roosters. The roosters gang-banged the poor hens. We had to lock the free-ranging fowl in our henhouse to protect them. Eventually, we rounded up most of the cocks. It was a bloody, stinking slaughter. Their meat was tough and gamey. Even when boiled for hours, my fricassee was inedible.

Winter that year was memorable for snow so deep we had to wear snowshoes to get from place to place. When the little boys walked the shoveled path from our cabin to the henhouse to feed the chickens and gather what eggs they could find, I saw only the red tassels of their stocking caps bobbing above the snow line. We decided to go to Seattle for a Christmas break. Evan, our neighbor down on Bear Creek, would feed the horses, the chickens, and the dogs and Siamese cat.

We returned to find the hens gone. A bobcat had broken through the screened window of the henhouse, killed all the chickens, and then settled in for a week to eat them one by one.

"I came up to feed them and there he was," said Evan. "Fat as a king. I took his picture. Figured the damage was done, so what the hell. May as well let him be."

The photo is blurry, but the marauder is clearly a bobcat. You can see his pointed, tufted ears, the spotted winter coat, slanted eyes, and white whiskers. All we could find of the prey were a few red combs and a dozen pairs of chicken feet.

This fall, some twenty-six years later, my second-oldest son, Steve, spotted two bobcats while hiking the ridge on Upper Bear Creek Road. He was with Betty.

"She treed them," he said. "She was all excited, barking and jumping at the tree. It was a larch, most of its needles gone. That's how I could see they were cats. I looked up and there were two round faces looking down at me. They were much bigger than Rascal [our chunky, neutered tiger cat], the larger one maybe thirty pounds. Their fur blended in with the tree—a golden color. I could see the spots. They didn't make a sound or flinch. Stared me straight in the eye."

I was jealous. How many times had I passed that tree and never caught a glimpse of bobcats?

—

This spring, I chat with my carpenter neighbor, Dan, who is driving his pickup through our place to cut firewood from slash piles left by Plum Creek's loggers.

"Never seen so much timber coming off those hills," I say. "It's been log trucks all day, every day for months. I don't dare go walking up in the high country. Upsets me too much."

As the logging increases, my parameters for roaming get more and more constricted. Sometimes I feel I'm in jail. Habitat destroyed, I walk tight, angry circles like a lion in a zoo. That may sound silly to an urban person for whom 163 acres of grass and trees seems as big as Central Park, but it's a fact of life for me. After living in solitude for so long, I felt put upon when someone built a house at the edge of our meadow—windows that glare into my space like a foreign person standing too close, making me jumpy, breathing garlic into my face.

"Took three days," says Dan, "for three sawyers to cut thirty-seven acres down to bare ground up toward Olson Peak. Just about made me cry. By the way, did you know you've got some mountain lions up there, above those cliffs?"

He was pointing at the only patch of tall timber left in my vicinity, a quarter-section of state-owned land that rises on a steep grade just south of my borders. Mountain lions need large, isolated, game-rich hunting grounds to survive. I lease that land for grazing and protect it as if it were mine, not part of the so-called industrial forest ruled by a succession of increasingly hungry timber corporations.

"That's where I saw the tracks of a big cat," I say.

"Young ones," Dan continues. "Three of them."

Dan believes we are seeing more mountain lions because trophy hunters are killing off the prize males. Mature males are loners, often slaughtering kittens in their hunting territory, thus quelling competition and keeping the population in check. With the big daddies dead, unschooled youngsters proliferate.

"Loss of habitat," I counter, "is another explanation for more lion sightings and attacks."

As western Montana becomes the last resort for "white flight" families, movie stars, and the more hardy variety of retirees, new housing developments are pushing into the wild woods and mountain slopes where lions dwell. What's a young lion to do when easy prey presents itself in his territory? A wandering poodle, for instance, or an overfed housecat; a plump toddler alone in the yard; a jogging woman who sets off his predator instinct, looking for all the world like a wounded doe.

"The problem's an explosion of people," I say, "not an explosion of wildcats."

I open the gate so Dan can pass through.

"Good thing we had an open winter. Should be a nice batch of fawns," he says, "and the elk'll be calving. No shortage there as far as I can see. That'll keep 'em busy."

———

Watching Dan's red pickup disappear into the Bear Creek watershed, I scan the meadow, which is dotted with mother cows and tender calves. There is no love in me for cows, but the calves, like all babies, are endearing. Moments like these I cannot help feeling protective of calves and fawns and spindly-legged newborn elk. Yet I am equally drawn to the mountain lions, who also must feed their young.

Nature is not confused by the mixed moral messages that perplex our self-reflective species. There is no pity in the world of eat-and-be-eaten. What I learn from the more-or-less wild place in which I live is respect for the beauty and logic of its interconnected parts.

There is new grass in April, berries in fall for deer and bear. Snipe build nests on the ground, and some nestlings feed owls and coyotes. To love the spotted fawn implies love for the wolf. Wildcats have killed my chickens, a housecat, perhaps even Little Red Dog, who loved to chase deer in the wild woods. We take our chances. I will walk again this evening. Three lions live on the cliff. They are sleek, invisible, ready to pounce.

Plainchant
for the Panther

by Jeffery Smith

1.

For months—this was some years ago—a solitary panther had stalked my dreams: a tawny smudge tracing through the laurel hell on the streambank right up the creek from the cabin where I lived, the tail snaking behind like wood smoke. The panther stayed silent, its eyes socketed in their pinioned trackings, clapped to my brow and flashing through the dark. It returned night after night, and I wanted to know what it was trying to tell me. The books and the biologists claimed that the last official panther sighting in the North Carolina mountains was in 1886. But over a century later, my neighbors still told stories to the contrary. So I went off into the Black Mountains, seeking panther sign. I took to walking barefoot in the woods up Swannanoa Creek. I felt the breath, the pulse, and the caesura, of the earth coming up through my feet. I craved bare contact and raw footsoles; for a long while I had lived deep into my misery, so self-absorbed and isolated that it took such measures to awaken me. I left my animal scent in scrapes and rockpiles; my feet traced bloody kisses across the crusted snow.

I took to the mountaintop behind my house. From that spot I had a panoramic view. I shawled myself in a blanket and sat still all night. That ridgetop is miles from any city, and the moonless sky was beswirled, animate with stars; it was hard to believe it held any blackness. The Milky Way showed itself plain, like some concave envelope into the beyond. I studied the stars overhead; I repeated to myself the animal names we've imposed on that panoply to lend some order to the night skies. She-bears and scorpions and swans hold up the heavens.

It was the story animal I was seeking. I sat supplicant on my knees beside a twig fire until finally I caught the scent of wild animal worrying its edges; the glint of my fire flared its eyes, and like coals those eyes gave back the fire.

Next day there was no sign of any animal there, so perhaps I imagined all this. No matter. Alchemy—which, as I understand it, is what happens when matter is imbued with spirit—starts with some image that guides us when we won't trust the invisible. Even a stiffened, locked-up soul can be invaded by grace, and I hung a little unhinged from that night forth; I am a little unhinged still. That night I finally knew: those eyes were just the sign I needed. The vertical pupils are a passageway beyond the self. The yellow iris strobes the heavens.

2.

In Kentucky, in 1770, Daniel Boone saw a panther "seated upon the back of a large buffalo"—this would have been an eastern woods bison, soon to be extinct, a little smaller than the western species but still outweighing the panther by about 1,500 pounds—with its claws "fastened into the flesh of the animal wherever he could reach it until the blood ran down on all sides." According to Boone's *Autobiography*, the plunging, rearing, and running of the bison "were to no purpose. The panther retained its seat and continued its horrid work." The legendary frontiersman found himself so unnerved by the sight that he could barely still his hand to shoot the panther dead.

This is one of the first recorded panther sightings by a white North American; to this day, few have seen a cougar stalk and kill. Yet it is mostly their "killing" that we talk about when we talk about panthers. In 1827, Major C. H. Smith described the "abstracted ferocity" of a feeding cougar trapped near his encampment that was shot immediately after it was fed: "The first ball went through his body, and the only notice he took of it was by a shrill growl, doubling his efforts to devour his food, which he actually continued to swallow with quantities of his own blood until he fell."

In 1851, Major John C. Cremony, traveling along the Pecos River in New Mexico, watched from a cautious distance as a puma "tore open the back" of a grizzly bear and "ripped at its vital organs until it died." In 1890 one W. A. Perry, a homesteader in Idaho, claimed that he had seen a cougar kill a "good-sized Indian pony and its colt, and drag them across a meadow and over a high fence into the adjoining woods." And near Glade Park, Colorado, in 1922, a single puma killed 192 bedding ewes in a single night and disappeared into the darkness without eating a one.

But consider this: John James Audubon's *Viviparous Quadrupeds of North America* tells us that sometime in the 1830s, "an old resident of South Carolina" saw a panther resting comfortably in a meadow near the present-day city of Greenville; all about this panther a half-dozen deer grazed, apparently—but this seems unlikely—unaware of his presence. Among the Creek Indians in the Southeast, the Deer and Panther Clans modeled their comportment after their namesakes. The clans were friendly with one another, except at dusk—the time of day, they knew, when panthers are most likely to hunt a deer—when they were forbidden to speak. We say "killing." But is that the right word? The she-panther is getting her meat, we might say instead: she is feeding her family. We say "ferocity," but what is that to a cougar? We say "victim," but is that what the deer thinks of itself?

To see a constellation more clearly, you tilt back your head and look away a bit; some distances are bridged only by indirection. And maybe we should turn our heads likewise when we consider the other animals, and allow some poetry to enter our understanding. Our great sadness is that our purported mastery of nature has so diminished animals in our consciousness that we can't see that panthers and deer are not "enemies"; no animal in all of creation is ever so simple. "Every creature," said Meister Eckhart, "is a word of God." In their skins animals bear witness to living in faith: they dwell content with their place in the order of things; they trust in the mystery that creation is to every creature. They are an ark of messengers about a universe not made by us.

So if a panther stalks a deer and then crouches into the killing haunch, and the deer smells the panther, it will likely flee. But that is only one behavior among many that these animals might carry on with one another. Any other time—you might see this on your next casual stroll in the forest—unless the big cat crouches, the deer might just lie out in the sun, in the same meadow with the panther, and calmly browse the grass.

3.

And what, anyway, is the value of skin? The bestiaries tell us that medieval Christians believed the skin of the lion bestowed on its wearer "divine linkages and celestial correspondences." Shamans of Pacific Northwest nations shook puma paws over their sick to drive forth evil spirits. Many Indian nations used the

hides—for the hunting powers they believed them to contain—
to quiver their arrows; George Catlin's 1840 portrait of Mah-to-
tah-pa shows the great Mandan warrior's prized puma-skin
quiver. In the 1850s, Plains Indians would swap eight buffalo
robes for a single cougar skin, to be used for ornamentation and
in sacred ceremonies. Forty years later a puma hide would fetch
just fifty cents from a white fur trader. A couple of decades later
a cougar "scalp" would fetch you a $50 bounty from ranchers in
any of the western states. Today in the American West, every
winter sport hunters shoot more than 2,000 cougars. Most of the
hides wind up in the trash.

We are covered by flesh, but how much does it contain us? I
want to believe that we can haunt other shapes, cast different
shades, ride our warm mammalian blood across specific boundaries. When an eighteenth-century New England Christian cult
received a divine message to do whatever they pleased, they
threw off their clothes and ran about giving animal calls. Think
of it: animal tracks are the oldest storytellers we know. Imagine
our earliest ancestors bent over some slough divining the meaning of that first alphabet: the tracks there in the mud. The other
animals inspired—in the literal sense of that word, they breathed
into our kind—our first metaphors, our first paintings, our first
gods. And animals grace our dreams, offering us skins and
masks and aliases for our long-hobbled dance across creation;
with them we might begin to move beyond whatever is merely
personal. We imagine ourselves into animal skins to remind us
that in all of creation there is nothing unique to humans: each
animal offers us some special knowledge for reimagining ourselves. One animal shape leads to another, and we begin to trust
in something larger than ourselves: the web of creation that links
every being.

To swap this—the possibility of "divine correspondences and
celestial linkages"—for any sum of cash shortchanges creation,
shortchanges our souls.

4.

Most Christians believe that Jesus is the only mediator between God and the human world. For the Zuni Pueblos of the Southwest, the cougar carries prayers to the gods and delivers divine messages back to the people. Navajo sand paintings depict the cougar bearing to the people gifts of "conjure water" and other healing concoctions.

To the Cherokees in the southern Appalachians, the panther was Klandagi, the lord of the forest. And centuries ago the Cochiti Pueblos in New Mexico fashioned from stone two life-size puma effigies, still visible today at Bandelier, to stand midway between the heavens and their nearby village.

Such lines, holding the animism of aboriginal peoples over the "human-centered" Christian world view, are oft-heard today. So it is a surprise to learn that according to another medieval bestiary, "The True Panther" is "our Lord Jesus Christ, who snatched us from the power of the dragon-devil on descending from the heavens." The bestiary goes on: "On the third day, the Panther-Christ rose from sleep and emitted a mighty noise breathing sweetness." This sweet breath offered life to the other animals but had the power to "repel and slay the dragon-devil."

This is no vapor trail: we recognize this panther even as it stands with one foot on the earth and the other in the heavens. The Book of Job counsels us: "Ask the beasts, and they will teach you; the birds of the air, and they will tell you; or the plants of the earth, and they will teach you; and the fish of the sea will declare to you. Who among all these does not know that the hand of the Lord has done this?" All the animals inhabit a world as familiar—and as unknown—to us today as it was to medieval Christians and the Pueblo peoples of the Southwest: the world of sacred strangeness that offers us the necessary, frightening, and liberating shock of otherness. All we lack is faith. Already, we have all we need of divinity: we pray to sky-gods; we live beside earth-gods.

5.

My third winter in the West—I'd moved to the region because
the big cats certifiably still lived there—I was nightwalking in
the Rattlesnake Wilderness just outside of Missoula. The pines
spired dark and lovely above the snow. The half-moon rose. Just
before dawn, I stopped walking and flopped onto the snow. A
snowshoe hare skated across the snow, and it came to me: there's
a cougar out there somewhere stalking it, the golden eyes an
astral blaze in the dark lodgepole forest.

That half-moon quartered the southern sky, and the snow
sent back its golden light. My hair danced in the gas the stars give
off. I sprawled in the snow. In the north Orion spun farther west.
The Pleiades were fading and glinting across time, like oracles.
For many years, I knew then, I'd been mostly hollow. I needed
filling and shaping, weighting and balancing; in short, I needed
remaking. And now, as I lay out there in the Montana night, I
knew it would come. I trusted—and this was a new thing, so new
I couldn't name it then—I trusted that the weight I needed
would come in its own time, and I trusted that I could bear it.

But that's another story. On that January night I lay still on
the Montana snow and breathed, and I watched my steam rise,
braiding itself into the wind and taking on forms. Some were
dark, fugitives and fledglings and migrants, my dark familiars.
There was bile and there was phosphor; there was lead and there
was vapor. Some floated into the sky and tracked moonshadows
across Stewart Peak. And some stayed here, where it's warm. To
this day they circle in my blood. I bid them all: *fly true*. It was a
silly thing to do, but I couldn't resist: I made angels in the snow.
The wind gusted out of the north. All around my head
diaphanous wings of snow did pinwheel: out to sky, back to
earth. Out to sky, back to earth. Just like that. Over and over.

6.

I can't help but think of Job, and the Voice out of the Whirlwind.
Lately I've been reading about the scream of the panther.

Across the continent that scream is a commonplace in pioneer accounts, standing for the very terror of the night, of the wilderness, of this strange land. "The cougar's scream is wild and weird," wrote one early naturalist from the forests of the Midwest, "and not calculated to soothe the nerves of a night wayfarer on a lonely forest trail." Charles Mead, who heard a panther along the Cimarron River in Oklahoma Territory in 1899, wrote that hearing the cat's "unearthly" scream would "freeze the blood in one's veins and for an instant paralyze almost any form of man or beast." A Montana trapper wrote in 1928 that the panther's scream would "cause anyone who hears it to lose his composure. He will lose his hat, lock his snowshoes, and drop his cocked rifle."

That voice is so unsurpassing weird that the *Frontier Palladium* of Malone, New York, reported in its August 1, 1850, edition that upon hearing an odd noise in the area "some of our gray-haired fathers, who had heard the scream of the panther when the site of our village was a wilderness wild, came out to see whether that animal was coming to regain its dominions." These men were no doubt surprised when they discerned the source of that "scream": approaching their peaceful village at just that moment was no panther, but rather the very first steam locomotive to enter their area, its whistle wailing its arrival.

And late last century one Matthew Arbuckle, while plowing on his claim in western Missouri, about a mile from the Osage River, heard a terrible noise coming from the direction of the river. Certain that it was a panther, Arbuckle rode into town and assembled a posse of men and hounds to "go after the varmint." As the posse rode toward the river, they heard a faint repetition of the noise Arbuckle had reported. It was, sure enough, a new and terrifying sound.

The men reached the river shortly before nightfall without seeing any sign of a panther. They camped in a cave—locally known as the "Rock House"—on the riverbank, and the night passed without event, but at daybreak "that nerve-racking sound brought every man to his feet and set the hounds howling. The noise seemed to show that the monster was coming up the river and was near." The men shouldered their rifles and posted themselves behind the large cottonwoods on the river's bank. Four of them "were told off with orders to have their knives ready and to wade in if the lead had failed to stop the beast."

Near Rock House was one of the sharpest of the Osage's many curves and bends. Around the point—its "nerve-racking" steam whistle caterwauling—and into view came slowly the "monster": it was the *Flora Jones*, the first steamboat to ascend the Upper Osage.

———

You know the story: after a series of agonizing setbacks, Job bemoans his fate, his friends can't console him, and Job becomes insolent enough to suggest that God's ways aren't sufficiently comprehensible, let alone just, to have any meaning for humanity. And the Voice out of the Whirlwind—the standard divine entity in Old Testament theophanies—manifests and asks Job if he, or any other human, can begin to comprehend, let alone duplicate, the wonders and mysteries of the creation: "Wilt thou hunt the prey for the lion, or fill the appetite of the young lions, when they crouch in their dens, and abide in the covert to lie in wait? Doth the hawk fly by thy wisdom, and stretch her wings toward the south? Doth the eagle mount up at thy command and make her nest on high?"

———

Skeptics deny that the mountain lion makes any such sound; they assert that they have never heard this cat scream. This chorus is led by some men who might have known: the famous cougar hunters Jay Bruce of California, "Uncle Jim" Owen of Arizona, Jim DeLong of Utah, and S. N. Leek of Wyoming— who among them killed untold thousands of cougars as whites settled the West—all claimed that panthers do not scream.

The naturalist Franklin Welles Calkins had a simple explanation for this apparent anomaly: "Everywhere that the animal has been found," Calkins wrote in 1902, "it has happened to the first settlers to listen to the unrestrained and natural voice of the cougar, and everywhere this discerning cat has stilled that voice at the bark of their dogs and the crack of their rifles."

And those who have testified to it have yet to puzzle out what the panther's scream might signify: in his account of a journey across the Rocky Mountains in the 1830s, John K. Townsend wrote of hearing "the dismal distressing yell by which this animal entices its prey until pity or curiosity induces the prey to approach to its destruction." In 1860, George Suckley, a naturalist in Washington Territory, guessed that the puma's "shrill screams proceed from the animal's amatory conflicts and spiteful sanguinary courtships." Enos Mills, who heard it only thrice in his long years studying Rocky Mountain wildlife, speculated that on one occasion the cougar's scream was given by "a mother frantically seeking her young," and on the other two occasions the cry "was a wail, given by a lion calling for a mate slain by a hunter."

We will likely never know what the scream of the panther bespeaks. Maybe it means grief for a lost mate or kitten; maybe it is one of the ways a panther procures her food; and maybe it utters procreation, the urge to send life forth from the self and into the unforeseeable future. In any event the animal is both vessel and voice for the life force.

So are we. And given such voice, and such wonders all about us to praise and to fear, who wouldn't scream?

—

One adjective occurs over and again in these old anecdotes: the puma's voice, it is said, is "unearthly." Odd that this most terrestrial creature—whose native home once covered more of the Western Hemisphere than any other mammal save the human—should have an "unearthly" voice. In the Old Testament the divine presence scarcely manifested to humans except as an elemental force: as wind, or flood, or fire. Ancient texts indicated the divine being with the unpronounceable tetragrammaton—translated as "YHWH"—so that the human tongue might never utter the mystery. But even about our divinities we cannot abide much mystery, and so we chose to blaspheme, and we named it: God.

But there is hope: we still don't have a single name for this wild cat. This one species—*Felis concolor* to biologists everywhere—was in our common parlance once known by at least forty different names. Even today, its several given names—panther, puma, cougar, mountain lion, catamount—are believed by most Americans to represent different animals. And—be they unnameable, unearthly, or whirlwind—all these voices say the same thing: divinity is just that mystery that we humans can never entirely comprehend—that is, the ongoing creation. Between us and the rest of creation is a veil of incomprehensibility. That mystery is all we might know of divinity.

So I've given up trying to interpret these dreams, these gifts of moisture scribed into my own stiff story by the hand of mystery. When they come to me now, I ask these panther divinities to spare me my certainties, skin me to wakefulness, shimmer me to some new shape. After all, who can tell how prayer is answered? Who can divine the shapes of an apparition?

And the Bible tells us that Job—convicted at last of his arrogance, his doubt, and his presumption, restored by the Voice to an understanding of the humble human place in God's creation, and finally certain that his suffering—that is to say, his self—was the least of it, would speak no more. "What shall I answer thee?" he asks the Lord. "I lay my hand upon my mouth."

Triangle

by Ellen Meloy

You will know that I lived to tell the tale. But, for a moment, picture me standing in a patch of mustang clover with my back to a grove of incense cedars, my throat bared to 130 pounds of airborne mountain lion coming straight at me, her large round forefeet posed to deliver so forceful a blow that few prey can escape. One and one-eighth inches separated her canine teeth, a breadth that can precisely straddle the neck vertebrae of a mule deer, snapping its spinal cord in a single bite. Her tawny body extended a full six feet to tail's tip. Her amber stare, inexorably fixed on my own, held me immobile and utterly fascinated.

Midlunge the lion's head snapped around with a brutal jerk,

yanked taut by the chain that held her collar to an eyebolt on the floor of the open pickup bed. Her master laughed, leaned over the bed, and curled his arm around the cat's neck, stroking her soft, rounded ears. She stared at me, longing for my scent. He leered at me, telling me without words just how far he would go, whether or not I was willing. She is not the predator, I thought; he is. Help was thirty miles down the mountain. The only rescue in sight was this mountain lion, if only I knew how to use her, and she was his, although I sensed that, given a chance, she would betray him.

I lived alone on this remote slope of the Sierra with fifty-four books and a diamondback rattler that slept under an outhouse decorated with a calendar from the sixties showing small children in J. C. Penney clothes gazing lovingly at Jesus. The nearest neighbor occupied a fire lookout eight miles away as the crow flies. In my mind the place was a refuge. Others considered it odd for a woman in her twenties to spend a highly sociable age with so little human discourse. Some insisted that I was asking for trouble, as if the entire, never-ending supply of perverts from Los Angeles, several hundred miles away, were now marching toward this exact spot. Friends were not sure what to do, so occasionally they brought casseroles, as if my aloneness were an illness or a grieving. Both the friends and I loved the gesture but not the casseroles, which seldom made it up the rough mountain road intact. After they parked, my visitors scooped rice and cheese off their floorboards. It's okay, I consoled them, I don't have an oven.

Several times during the summer, strangers unfamiliar with the area took a wrong turn on the fire lookout road and came down the dirt track to my dead-end. They saw few signs of human presence. The cabin and my vehicle were not visible from the road. If I was not off hiking on the mountain, I hid from company, guarding my solitude or lacking the energy to be nice to anyone.

The cowboy with the mountain lion, however, knew this territory. He knew I lived here, although we had never spoken. He often drove up the valley to tend the cattle that grazed illegally inside the nearby national park. The park rangers never looked for the cows, the cows could not read the No Trespassing signs, and the cowboy did not care. He was lean and full of shadows and challenges. One day he brought me his mountain lion. He knew that the cat would draw me out.

"I found her in a den," he said.

Although I did not speak, he answered the obvious question and softened none of the details. He wanted me to believe, as he did, that the lion's loyalty to him ignored its price.

"Treed the mother with my dogs and shot her. I kept this one cub." He did not seem the type to have used a drown-the-kittens-in-a-bag technique on the rest of the litter. He had likely clubbed them with a rifle butt.

The lioness closed her eyes and rubbed her muzzle and ears against the snaps on his shirt as a housecat rubs a table leg. Her body curled in an upturned U-shape that had none of the liquid stretch and rolling bone of shoulder blades so typical of big cats. Relaxed after her leap at me, she sagged slightly, as if she had shrunk inside, leaving a limp cat skin outside. Her soft muscles convinced me that the man never let her run but routinely chopped up those illegal cows and fed them to her.

"Back home I keep her on a chain hooked to a wire clothesline so she can run its length." The mountain lion languished against him. "She keeps out the bikers and the Mexicans." He grinned, as if attempts on his life and property were common.

I was too young to deconstruct stereotype but not inexperienced in bigotry. I thought this behavior befitted someone who believed that a mountain lion would abandon her wild nature simply to feed his ego. Mountain lion, national park, me—all were his for the taking.

The image of the mountain lion pacing the clothesline made

me dizzy. In my mind I saw her moving back and forth beneath strands hung with towels and underwear. I saw myself unclipping the chain and levitating the neighbor children to safety as the cat loped off. The only mountain lion I had seen thus far was a dead one, a rib cage with bits of matted fur and a dry, thin skull with ambiguous lines. So rare is the sight of a mountain lion in the wild, I wondered if these might be the only encounters I would ever have: that corpse and this prisoner. I did not know that in the coming years, mountain lions would present themselves, one after the other, so that I would collect a lifetime of cats in the wild. The lions in my future would be hungrier than this one.

With no wild sightings yet in my experience, it was nearly impossible not to react to the mountain lion in the truck with interest and wonder and disdain, and emotion was what the man expected of me. Helping oneself to exotic pets was a waning tradition in these mountains, and the master predators fared the worst—wolves (while they lasted), coyotes, bears, mountain lions, foxes, golden eagles. Few bothered with bobcats, for they manifested a too-crazy, shrieking wild, like an overgrown housecat on amphetamines. A number of Sierra foothill ranchers were known to keep a coyote pup from their predator-control killings, and the stories shared a sad pattern. At first a source of amusement and novelty, the animals became a world of trouble, or a marginalized, diminished being in a kennel or tethered to a line, bored and pacing and chewing a fence to bits. My generation was now helping to turn apathy toward captive wildlife into widespread public scorn.

Ten feet from truck, man, and cat, I held my ground, ankles buried in mustang clover. Steller's jays scolded from the cedars, as they did when the resident black bear passed on the trail below the cabin. Jays were my alarm against any intruder, benign or threatening, into an otherwise serene world. Whenever I heard the birds, I lived a tug-of-war between safe quarter and aching curiosity. Their raucous, unceasing squawking did nothing to deter the man's aggression. He begged for my contempt so that he could laugh in my face. He wanted me to stroke this cat; he wanted me to note the difference in power between zookeeper and exhibitionist. I had no weapons save a demeanor of indifference. He thought it imperturbable and raised the stakes.

I might have ended the standoff by running. No swordsman leaped out of the bush and lopped off this man's genitals on my behalf. So I tried to believe that if he assaulted me, the lioness would be my ally and turn on him. Thus, each of the *Homo sapiens* in this triangle knew what he and she wanted. Neither of us knew what the mountain lion wanted. Humans bully other species because we seldom try to understand them. They seem to oblige us when we ask something of them, but their requests leave us blank or bewildered.

To discourage attack, some animals appear detached and oblique; they often avert their gaze. Before I could turn away, I again became a source of intense interest to the lioness. She caught my eye and froze her stare. I imagined myself inside her skin. When she knows I am greatly moved, I thought, she will act in a sympathetic manner.

Do it. I did not know if the voice was mine, asking for rescue, or hers, asking for revenge. Perhaps it was his voice, calling me over to place my bare and uncertain fingertips on her warm and beating heart.

Riding after Lion

by Verlyn Klinkenborg

Down in the canyon, the foxhounds are talking *Felis concolor*—mountain lion. To the minutest molecular remnant of cat—the vanishing trace of a pawprint on stone—each dog in the pack reacts with a pure, stricken note of acclaim that is many times larger than the dog itself. Even the young dogs, Ribbon and Rifle, have the knack. To say the pack "barks" or "bays" or "gives voice" suggests that the dogs must physically produce the vocal summons that comes from within them. But what appears to happen is this: the dogs open their mouths and show you the cry that inhabits them, a cry as full and abrupt as light, elicited only by lion. It is haunting. The echoes roll across Hog Canyon,

across the Peloncillo Mountains, and out over Arizona's San
Bernardino Valley—the Malpai borderlands—and then they
disperse at last almost within earshot of Mexico.

Where I sit—aboard a mule named Musket on a slope sheer
enough to make an updraft welcome—I can look the length of
the tawny spine of the Peloncillos and into the blue Sierra Madre
along the southern horizon, somewhere in Sonora or Chihuahua.
If I were to ride just a little higher, I could peer into Hidalgo
County, New Mexico. But from where I sit I'm able to gaze
nearly straight down upon the dogs and their owners, Warner
Glenn and Tommy Todd, who are tracking in an oak-shaded
draw several hundred feet below me. The men and hounds down
there are as tough and lean as a barbed wire gate, and so, in her
own feminine manner, is Kelly Glenn-Kimbro, Warner's daughter, who waits, radio in hand, .357 Magnum on hip, aboard a
mule called Dollar on the slope just above me. Warner, at sixty-
one, has been hunting deer and lions in this range since he was a
boy of eight. He learned the art of tracking from his father,
Marvin Glenn, who first began lion hunting to protect his livestock in 1938. Kelly, thirty-five, has been hunting and guiding
beside her father and her grandfather (before his death in 1991)
since she was able to ride, taking time off only for college and for
the birth of her daughter, Mackenzie. Tommy, who ranches near
Willcox, has been hunting and guiding with Warner and Kelly
for the last ten years. The dogs—well, with the dogs, of course, it
goes back centuries, even if some of them are only pups who still
run necked together with a short leather lead.

Warner and Tommy and the pack, ten foxhounds in all,
have returned to the last place they caught a strong whiff of
lion. Moments ago, they were high above our present position
on the canyon wall, following a scent that suddenly failed.
Moments before that, we were all riding peaceably along the
canyon floor together—in and out of the mid-November shade,
sometimes in the creekbed, sometimes on a ledge above it—

when the dogs caught the scent of lion and took off with Warner and Tommy hard behind them. We climbed out of the canyon with the pack, and now here we wait while they retrace their steps. There is no reason for us to move until we know which way the scent moves. That is the nature of lion hunting. One day it's nothing but new ground, a track that leads on and on, away from the trucks and the horse trailer and off into the night. The next day it's nothing but déjà vu, the track dying out and suddenly freshening, doubling back again and again, until some stretches of trail look familiar even to greenhorns.

—

Down in the canyon, eerily distant beneath me, Warner walks quickly, bending from time to time to examine the hard-packed sand in the creekbed, craning into the brush to scrutinize some anomaly in a pile of leaves. From my angle, his hat nearly hides him from sight. The dogs swarm ahead, quivering with attention, sifting the air through a pack full of nostrils. When Warner sees the right kind of something—a track, a scratch— he calls the dogs over and asks them their opinion, which they express unequivocally, yea or nay. (The dogs call Warner over if they find something interesting first.) With his own half of the pack, Tommy does the same thing a little higher up the slope. It looks, from where I sit, as though dog and man alike were searching thoroughly, if randomly, for a lost contact lens. Seen from this height, the hounds appear to have shed a dimension, to have flattened themselves—wriggling splotches of liver and white—against the foreshortened terrain. Sometimes Warner treads in the pool of his own shadow. Sometimes his shadow can barely keep up with him.

High on the slope where Kelly and the hunters wait, the mules are nearly silent, but not uninterested, as long as the dogs can be heard. The mules signal tersely to each other with their ears, and then, after a few moments of silence from below, they lapse into comas. The only sounds they make while lion hunting are the sounds of old leather flexing, the clatter of hooves against rock, of loose soil being dislodged on a steep trail, the scraping of juniper or manzanita branches against oiled chaps, and perhaps, at the very height of the climb, some labored breathing. But as the day goes on, their mulish irony becomes more and more apparent. If the cat track gives out or leads back along that morning's trail, they say nothing. If a hunter hangs up while scrambling into the saddle from the steep downhill side, they say nothing. Their silence is a joke they seem grimly to enjoy. There is no making friends with them, for, unlike horses, they aren't the least bit flirtatious. You can pretend to neck-rein them or plow-rein them, but the truth is that where a mule puts its tiny feet while lion hunting is none of your business. As Kelly says, "It's better not to look sometimes."

———

What she means is that lion hunting with the Glenns in the Coronado National Forest is not for the vertiginous. Climbing the sides of Hog or Baker or Sycamore Canyon on muleback is relatively easy, for a rising mule drives a rider deep into the saddle. And since a mountain lion is reasonably likely to travel upward when pressured, a good part of every day is spent going up. But sooner or later you run out of up. The mules emerge onto a windswept mountaintop savannah broken by yucca stalks and sacahuista and circular sand clearings made by ants. All that's left is the spectacle of an enormous desert basin spreading below you from the foot of Starvation Canyon to the Perilla Mountains, which lie just this side of Douglas, Arizona. (In the midst of that basin you can make out a slight shift in the color of vegetation near an isolated knoll: that is the Malpai Ranch, where Warner Glenn and his wife, Wendy, live.) Down is suddenly the inevitable choice, faith in mules the only gospel. It takes a day or two of riding straight downhill, leaning way back, feet forward, head almost resting on the mule's rump, before you realize, thankfully, that the human body won't fork any farther than it already does and that, if you use them, the groin muscles will take some weight off your knees and keep you from sliding over the saddle horn and the mule's head and down to a precipitate perdition among the sun-beaten rocks below. By day's end, you feel as though you've ridden as far vertically as you have horizontally, and you're nearly right. A hunter named Leroy, a team-roper from Texas, put the matter succinctly. "I ride a lot," he said in a tobacco-dark voice, "but I ain't never rode like this before."

And here, parked side-slope on Musket, a raven's flight above Warner Glenn, who is stooped beside a day-old cougar track—something he knows because a spider has had time to dig a hole in the depression left by one of the lion's digits—I find myself thinking, as I do every morning here, about the matter of hunting and probability. The thought is prompted by the expanse of country that falls within my sight, an enormous mountain corridor traveled by perhaps twenty-five to thirty lions, who move constantly, individually, along its length, paying no heed to borders. That is a large number of cats, as many as the range can hold, and yet so furtive are they, so seldom seen by chance, and so extensive their overlapping territories that it seems almost presumptuous to ride into this country with the stated intention of seeing one, much less shooting one. Hunters' success often depends upon chance, but what it really depends upon is their ability to reduce the influence of chance, to raise the probability of encountering their prey. Hunting is often mistaken for the moment when game at last comes into view and the shot is fired or the arrow loosed or the photograph taken. But hunting is really the skillful effort to lessen improbability in the highly contingent world of nature.

———

The odds against my riding a mule into the Peloncillo Mountains and tracking and treeing a lion by myself are almost incalculable. (In fact, the odds against my being able, if required, to find my solitary way back to the truck are too high for comfort.) Warner's already decent chances of finding a lion are hugely improved by the presence of the dogs, and yet the dogs' chances of trailing a lion for any distance—except on a very hot scent— are similarly improved by Warner's presence: the dogs read only odor, after all, not visible sign. The likelihood of finding a lion is also greatly enhanced by the fact that, with Tommy and Kelly here, we can cover more ground by splitting up, one party cutting high across the shoulder of a canyon, for instance, while another party rides along the canyon floor. Weigh all these factors together, and two conclusions emerge. The first: Given enough time—and five days is almost always enough—it's virtually certain that Warner Glenn will find a lion in the Peloncillos. The second: As long as Musket and I stay healthy and keep up with the pack, my presence has no bearing whatever on the outcome of the hunt, the probability of finding a lion. To believe otherwise is superstition or vanity. It's a chastening thought and, at the same time, oddly liberating.

But what this chain of dependencies ultimately depends on, of course, is the character of the cat himself—that feline insouciance and that equally feline distaste for protracted exertion. A tom lion in the Malpai borderlands is likely to travel a long circuit, perhaps 250 miles, and to do so in the space of a week or ten days. But when it has made a fresh kill—deer, most often— or come upon a receptive female, it's unlikely to move very far at all. And when the hounds are on its heels, a lion is likelier to hole up or tree up or turn and face the dogs on a precipice, than to try and outrun them over a long distance. In fact, I wondered why a lion is ever caught in the Peloncillos until I saw Warner and Tommy and Kelly cover country afoot with the dogs. The Peloncillos aren't tall mountains, but they are rugged. The high terrain looks almost impenetrable, a rimrock precinct full of good hiding spots. But there's hardly any place a pack of foxhounds can't get to, even if Warner has to lower the dogs, one by one, off a ledge or down a chute. And where the dogs can't go, Warner and Tommy and Kelly can.

—

If I were a lion, I decided, I'd wait until I saw the Glenn hunting party ride up the trail at dawn, and then I'd spend the day sleeping in the sun on top of the horse trailer. But to say that misses the essential, proprietary swagger of a mountain lion. If I were really a lion, I would do exactly what one big tom lion did on the fifth day of this hunt—the 24th of November—the day Warner and Kelly and Leroy treed him. I would saunter, unconcerned, down an open trail on the ridge between Hog Canyon and Dry Skeleton Canyon—a trail full of human and dog scent, where Kelly's husband, Kerry Kimbro, and I (the human I, that is) had stood beside a burning sacahuista during a hailstorm the day before. I (the lion) would wind up walking smack into Warner Glenn, a mule named Snowy River, and a hound named Pistol. I would run a ways, cut into some difficult country, and, in the end, find myself treed, shot, and posing as a lion-skin rug beside a baby named Mackenzie who will, with good luck and wise land management, become the fourth generation of lion-hunting Glenns.

—

I—the human I—was obliged, of course, to catch a plane from Tucson after four days of hunting and so missed all the excitement of the fifth day, and with it some share of the remorse that is inseparable from the lives of thoughtful hunters. The hunt that ended that day had begun, five days before, the first hunt of the season, in a slightly reluctant mood. We wanted only to see a lion, we all agreed. And yet, thinking of his livestock and the diminished Malpai deer herd, as well as the balance of the lion population, Warner said, "If we come across some old tom that needs shooting, we'll sure go ahead and shoot him." It had become almost a joke, after two days of very hard riding, to say that any animal that put us through so much pain in its pursuit deserved to be shot, although with a little twist of that logic we might well have murdered the mules. There were false trails— that of a female with kittens, for instance—as well as day-old tracks and tracks that the dogs picked up at the long end on the wrong end of the day. The air and soil were unusually dry for November, and the scent wouldn't hold. The dogs caught it clearly only where a lion had crossed solid rock. But by the fourth day, we had pretty much triangulated a sizable sector of the Peloncillos, which meant that the hunters had seen some glorious country and that Warner had made a fix on the movements of several cats. It meant, too, that the operations of chance were steadily diminishing.

———

On that fourth morning, I was riding up a corner of Hog Canyon with Warner and his son-in-law, Kerry, when the dogs hit a fresh scent. Just as they covered it, and the ancient peal of hounds rang out, an inexplicable rain began to fall, accompanied by hail and lightning. Whatever track the cat had laid was quickly washed away. But its meaning was plain. Riding out of the canyon mouth that afternoon under a clear, dry sky, Warner turned to me and said, "I believe we'll go up Hog Canyon again tomorrow morning. I believe that old tom will be up there."

Warner was wearing the remains of a Carhartt jacket bleached white by the sun and shredded by the acacia and ocotillo thorns that pluck at a rider in this desert country. His heavy leather chaps lay astraddle the saddle horn, as they do every day once the hunting gets serious and he begins to work on foot with the dogs, running beside them in worn-out hunting boots and spurs. He is quick to laugh and quick to joke. (When I asked him at dinner that night how to spell "sacahuista," he paused and said, "Exactly like it sounds, Verlyn.") He has a long, weathered, highly expressive face. There's a look he makes when he turns around in his saddle to see who's been left behind on the trail, and one he makes when he whistles to the dogs, and still another when he lets out a whoop to call the dogs in, using the canyon walls to carry his voice down into the cracks and crevices. And, as I saw at that moment, riding beside him up the road to the horse trailer, there's also a look Warner makes when the guesswork has gone out of hunting. Knowledge carries with it a certain weight, and it was possible to see it then in Warner's eyes.

That morning, like every morning at the Malpai Ranch, we had eaten breakfast at 4:30, and it was perhaps ten to five by the time we got down to the barn. Orion was cartwheeling toward the southwestern horizon, and Venus lay hidden behind the Peloncillos. There was not a trace of the coming day in the sky, only a faint, livid glow, like the gloom of a bad conscience, coming from the western sky beyond the Malpai, above Douglas, population 16,000, and its sister city, Agua Prieta, Mexico, just across the border, population 116,000. A strong light burned at the ranch house up the hill, and a set of lamps shone in the tack room, casting a broken pallor over the corrals and the hay shed. The mules stood saddled at the edge of the darkness, waiting to be bridled and loaded on the trailer. Their breath hung motionless in the cold morning air. From the kennels came the appalling clamor of twenty-one foxhounds vying for Warner's attention, a succession of blue notes colliding in the blackness. One by one the mules stepped into the trailer, reins draped across their necks, and one by one ten chosen dogs leaped, or were lifted, into the back of Warner's pickup, where they lay huddled together beneath a canvas canopy.

—

There was something about the way the humans crowded around the pickup's open doors in the dark—checking pistols and radios by the dome lamp—that made the darkness seem even larger than it had when we first walked out the back door of Wendy Glenn's kitchen after breakfast. Riding after lion had made it easier to imagine the true quantity of darkness lying out there in the Malpai borderlands. The night before, just at sunset, we had trailed single file over a saddle in the Peloncillos and down onto their western slope, looking out over the desert where Warner and Wendy and a few other ranchers run their cattle and make their homes. Each ranch is a fastness of its own, protected by bad roads and mesquite, by the sheer difficulty of ranching there—and protected too by the watchfulness of neighbors in a place where neighbors are scarce. The ranches are so few, and so girdled by brush and immured by the irregular topography of the valley floor, that they virtually disappear into the desert. When we paused on the saddle to look down at the last of the sunset—a broad bar of clouds dividing the sky, a warm moon rising behind us—there was not a light shining anywhere as far as we could see, forty miles and more to the west and the south and the north. Had we ridden down the eastern slope of the Peloncillos, the same thing would have been true.

—

There were more people, homesteaders and prospectors alike, in the Malpai—between the Perilla and Chiricahua Mountains in Arizona and the Big Hatchet and Alamo Hueco Mountains in New Mexico—at the turn of the century than there are now. To most of those early settlers, it seemed quite natural to try to extirpate lions from the country, just as it did to extirpate Indians and wolves and grizzlies and jaguars. The grizzlies are gone, and so, almost certainly, are the wolves, but so, too, are most of the settlers, extirpated in turn by the forces that have sucked the vast majority of Americans toward the cities during the past century. What remains is a wild, open country full of the surprises that nature provides when such a harsh terrain falls empty, for the most part, of human malevolence and what sometimes pass for good intentions. In the first week of March 1996, Warner Glenn found himself on the track of an animal that left a heavier footprint than a lion leaves, the digits more oval and more widely spread, the stride a little different. When he caught up with it on the edge of a cliff near Red Mountain, after a chase that began on a ridge in Hog Canyon, he found himself face to face with a jaguar (*Panthera onca*), something that in more than sixty years of hunting in the Malpai neither he nor his father had ever seen, though they had often talked of the possibility. Warner got some snapshots and dragged the dogs away long enough to allow the jaguar to make its escape.

To some, I suppose, this is a region full of ghosts, particularly those of the Chiricahua Apaches and their leader, Geronimo, who surrendered to General Nelson Miles in the Peloncillos just a century ago. To the Glenns, it is a region full of memories, of Marvin Glenn, especially, and of a succession of hounds and horses and mules and lions and of the events that have woven them all together, season by season. It seems, now, when I think about the slow drive we took each morning through the waning darkness, up into the Peloncillos or down a narrow track into the brush at their base, that we were preparing to hunt something not entirely phenomenal, something that could not quite be grasped with the senses. It was impossible to ride with Warner and Kelly without understanding that the country had been changed for them forever by that brief encounter with a jaguar. They showed me where the jaguar had run, but I could not imagine it because to me the presence of lions themselves in the Peloncillos still felt almost ghostly. I saw the lion tracks. I peered deep into the shadows beside Kelly and I saw the square a lion etches in the soil when he is scratching. Perhaps if I had been in at the kill that fifth day, had felt the warmth still in the lion's fur, the weight of his head in my hands, the still-supple musculature under the skin, it might have felt less insubstantial. But by then what we were hunting—something truly insubstantial, after all—would have departed from the lion anyway.

By the time we park the trailer, there is a broad rim of orange along the edge of the Peloncillos, and the sky has begun to pale overhead. The mules come out of the trailer the same way they went in, with unexpected dignity and professionalism. We tighten their cinches, hang canteens from the saddle horns, stuff lunches into the saddlebags, put on chaps, and mount. There is a pause. I wonder what the lions in the Peloncillos are doing at that moment. Then the tailgate drops and the dogs spill onto the ground like running water. They will soon know.

San Pedro Lion

by Warner Glenn

About 7 A.M. on a still-cool summer morning, John Cook and I
rode north from the Malpai ranch headquarters with a couple of
John's friends, intending to show them a piece of Arizona's San
Bernardino Valley. I've lived here all my life, ranching and guiding mountain lion hunts.

Ten minutes out, my wife's voice crackled on the radio. A
lady from Cascabel, on the San Pedro River, had called to say
that a good cow dog had just been killed by a mountain lion. I
told Wendy to let the caller know I'd come up that day, and
asked her to phone my daughter and best hand Kelly, to see if
she could go with me to check it out.

A couple of weeks before, some friends in the Cascabel area had mentioned that goats and household pets had been disappearing, including at least seventeen dogs. They had told their neighbors to call me the next time an animal came up missing.

We continued our ride up to the top of Steer Pasture Mountain; then, as we started back to the ranch, my mind traveled ahead to the lion situation. John asked what I was planning to do, and when I told him, he asked if he could go along. I was happy to have his company and help.

We loaded three mules, eight dogs, canteens, and some food, picked up Kelly, and drove to the ranch where the cow dog, Banjo, had vanished. Ranch hands Jorja Foster and Ray Gamez were there to meet us when we arrived around 2 P.M.

A drag mark led through the soft, dusty corral into dense mesquite thicket leading toward the river. The drag mark left by the dog's body and the distinct tracks of a big tom lion on both sides of the drag were very plain: the lion had straddled his kill, dragging the dead dog between his legs. Most of the time when you go in on a kill, things aren't this clear, this quick.

We followed the drag about 200 yards into thick weeds and brush before we lost it. It had rained a little the night before, and rain marks on top of the lion tracks and drag marks placed the time of the kill sometime before 11 P.M. the previous day. Even that slight amount of rain had completely erased any scent the dogs might be able to follow.

It would be hard to find Banjo in this mesquite jungle, but we unloaded the eight dogs, necking six together in pairs for easier control, and took them back to where the drag marks faded out. The dogs couldn't smell anything, so we worked toward the river, hoping the hounds would wind the kill and hit some fresher lion sign to follow.

Kelly and Jorja took the center position, walking toward the river through the mesquite, while John and Ray headed toward the river on the right flank. I took the dogs through on the left flank, upriver. I had covered the half-mile to the river's edge when John came on the radio to report lion tracks on the river's edge, apparently crossing over. Then Kelly radioed that she and Jorja had also picked up lion tracks heading downriver.

Working my way down to the others, I hadn't gotten far when two of my dogs broke off to investigate a very secluded, dark and shady part of the thicket. The dogs weren't barking, but they were very interested in a certain spot. I went to them and saw Banjo lying in dense shade, on a green carpet of ferns and small weeds. The lion had ripped out a portion of his shoulder and neck and had torn into the chest cavity, consuming the dog's heart and part of his lungs. He had made no attempt to bury or hide his kill, though I was sure he planned to come back that night to eat more of the still-fresh meat.

I've seen a lot of lion kills, but the sight of a cowboy's good cow dog, friend, and pet lying there so still gave me a very strange, sad feeling. Banjo's eyes were closed. His lips were pulled back, mouth shut, front legs crossed. Near the gaping hole, blood was smeared on his neck and shoulder, but his coat was still snow-white on the hind parts and even on his head, with its black ears.

My dogs Bawlene and Bud, very much alive and interested, seemed unable to comprehend the sight of one of their own so lifeless. I found the other dogs, Klump and Krackle, not barking but very interested in some scent on the underside of leaves and twigs that the lion had touched as he moved away from the kill. When I reached Kelly and Jorja at the river's edge, we studied the lion tracks in the sand and mud and determined that they were made after the rainfall. The dogs could now pick up scent, but it still wasn't strong enough to bark on.

We joined up with John and Ray and saw where the lion had made a ten-foot jump across the small stream and scrambled up the bank on the other side.

The dogs were able to trail to some extent by smelling the

brush, but they weren't barking, making it hard for me to keep them in sight. It was about 3 P.M. by now, and very hot. The night's rainfall had evaporated, taking with it the scent from tracks on the ground, but there was still enough scent left on the limbs and leaves to start the dogs tracking.

I told Kelly and John to get the mules, my pistol, and some food, then work the river's east side. I would keep them posted on where I was going with the dogs on the west side. Jorja and Ray would go back to the ranch and wait.

Heading downriver through the thick brush, I was relieved to catch up with a couple of the dogs. It worries me when they aren't barking, when I can't see them or hear them panting. I know they're getting a faint smell and moving on, though I think, "Dad-gum-it! I should've stayed right on their tails!" In this case, I knew they were going the right way from the kill and didn't think the lion would be too far away.

As late as we'd gotten there, I thought we'd be lucky just to find the kill—then we would try early the next morning to catch the lion. But we'd found the kill fast, and it was a big, heavy lion. We had three or four hours of good light left, so there might be a chance of finding the lion yet this afternoon.

Walking downriver with the dogs leading the way, I came to where a large canyon, La Minita, also known as Soza Canyon, opens onto the river. The tracks led up Soza, and in about a quarter of a mile, I saw more lion tracks leading up and down the canyon. It was hard to tell which way the lion had gone last, but since the tracks went up only so far, it became fairly clear that he had gone up the canyon and then back down a ways, turning out somewhere.

Both sides of Soza Canyon are rimmed with almost vertical rock bluffs and cliffs, with only a few places a man or dog could climb out. After a thorough search of both sides of the canyon bottom, the dogs couldn't find where the lion had gone up and neither could I. It was frustrating for all of us to be that close and not know which way to turn. The dogs and I were ready to try something else, so I decided to climb out on the canyon's north rim. Dogs are wonderful because no matter what you decide to do or which way you want to cut, they go right along and don't try to do your thinking for you.

When we got out on top of the ridge, Krackle and Bud started barking on a large lion track going off into the next canyon to the north.

Kelly and John had brought the mules to the junction of the San Pedro River and Soza Canyon and were waiting for word on which way to go. They had found a lot of older tracks in the mud along the river's edge, but nothing very fresh. I raised them on the radio, letting them know what the dogs were doing and what I'd found so far. I told them to stay there a little longer; then I left the ridge top and caught up with the dogs, who were trailing down the small canyon north of the ridge. They trailed it pretty good for a ways, then lost the trail again.

I *knew* the lion had turned out, but the ground was so rocky and hard that I couldn't find tracks, and the scent was still too dim for the dogs to find. I had started cutting one side of the canyon with the dogs, looking for clues, when I noticed two ravens squawking and diving in the air on the ridge I had just crossed, about a quarter of a mile up. I could see them climb; then they dove out of sight behind the ridgeline.

This rang a bell in my brain. I've seen ravens dive and scream at lions on bluffs in the past, and wondered if our tom lion might be lying on a ledge just over the ridge. Or the ravens could just be playing—scolding a deer or javelina. Once again, the dogs were ready to move on and try something else, so we all made our way toward the top.

Krackle, who was ahead of me, reached the top and went over. The other dogs were spread out to my right and left and a couple were coming behind. Krackle hadn't been out of sight for ten seconds when I heard her let out the damnedest screaming howl I've ever heard a dog make. Instantly, the rest of the pack stampeded in her direction, over the top. She'd either been charged by a javelina hog—or been attacked by that lion.

I had about 100 yards more to go up the steep slope when I heard the rest of the dogs open up with frantic, steady baying. Even though I couldn't see, I knew what was happening: the dogs were holding tight with the dog-killing lion at bay.

My legs were aching and my lungs were burning as I tried to reach the top, where I'd be able to see. I realized I didn't even have my pistol with me. When I was about twenty steps from the top, I heard the dogs pull out and head toward the San Pedro. That old lion had ducked away to find a safer spot to make his stand.

———

Although I hadn't seen it, I could picture the scene in my mind:

Krackle trots over the ridge, nose close to the ground in search of fresh lion scent. Tom Lion lies in the shade of a ledge, disturbed by the two diving ravens, but resting and watching out of survival instinct. Something moving over the ridge catches his eye—a white dog sniffing slowly along toward him. His first thought is, "Well, I'll be damned—here comes supper."

When Tom Lion made his charge, this white dog turned into a Walker hound that had been making her living over the past several years by dodging such charges and turning the situation around.

After the missed charge the lion thought, "No problem, I'll get her this next time." Then he saw several more dogs come over the ridge, called by Krackle's furious barking. Thinking it was raining dogs, he decided to head to the river, where the trees were a whole lot higher.

———

I radioed Kelly and John that we'd jumped the lion and he was headed to the river. "Get on those mules and head downriver as fast as you can, and bring me my gun."

Running in the direction the dogs had gone, I soon heard them again, this time barking treed. As I came within sight of the dogs, the lion, perched high on a limb, saw me. Making eye contact, he immediately started down the tree to within fifteen feet of the ground, jumped out over the dogs, and hit the ground running toward the dense growth along the river's edge. Kelly and John, coming downriver, radioed to say they could hear the dogs.

Next time I caught up, the dogs were barking at the base of a large tree only thirty yards from the river's edge. I thought the lion would probably stay put since he was breathing heavily and was high enough to feel secure. A couple of minutes later, Kelly and John came crashing through the mesquite on foot. They had left the mules some ways back due to the dense brush.

Kelly handed me my pistol belt and took some pictures of the treed lion. I was buckling the pistol belt around my waist, not watching the lion, when Kelly said, "Dad, you'd better shoot that thing—he's going to leave."

I looked up to see the lion moving out on the limb. I pulled out my pistol, aimed, and squeezed. The lion flinched as it jumped into the middle of the dogs and died running, about thirty yards out.

We dressed out the big tom and studied the contents of his stomach, determining that his last meal had been a white dog named Banjo. There were also some interesting bits of nylon and plastic strips in his stomach that really had me stumped. After studying these for a moment, John said, "I'll bet these are bits of a flea collar," and I believe he was absolutely right. Banjo hadn't been wearing a flea collar, but something in the last few days had been, and it remained in the lion's stomach undigested. Maybe someone's pet housecat.

This was a big lion, perfectly healthy, that appeared to be in the prime of life. Why he'd opted for a diet of household pets, I don't know.

We tied the lion behind the saddle atop my mule, Dollar, and headed back to the Cascabel ranch.

I have hunted lion most of my life. We hunt lion for trophy—

some you kill and some you don't, only photographing them and enjoying them. Once in a while, you find one that needs killing. The "San Pedro Lion" needed to go. He had picked up some habits over his seven or eight years that were strange and not too good. He had lost his respect for and fear of people and had learned to live in close proximity to their dwellings. He had taken dogs out of doghouses, from porches, and off runs in people's yards.

This could have turned into a dangerous situation had the opportunity presented itself. Imagine a small child playing in his or her yard late in the evening and the tom lion just happening by and happening to be hungry. That would be terrible for the family and the child, and just as terrible for the cat, because it would paint an untrue picture of the mountain lion. I think we may have kept him from making a real bad name for himself.

All in all, it was a very interesting day—though for me the best part was the ride back to Malpai in the pickup with my daughter and friend, talking about what the day had brought.

Lion Story

by Rick Bass

A mountain lion once chased Colter down an old logging road. It was in the summertime and we were just out hiking, climbing the mountain above the cemetery. Colter got a ways out ahead of me, galloping—charging up that mountain, only a year-old dog but already as powerful as a draft horse, as graceful as a thorough-bred—and after a little while, I heard him yelping excitedly, as he often did when he flushed a grouse by accident.

His nose was forever leading him to grouse.

There was a silence after that. I assumed he was chasing the flyaway bird, an act I hoped to discourage, and I shouted, "Colter, *leave* it!"

I was standing on the slope of the roadcut above the old grown-over logging road. Presently I heard the cyclonic thump-pattering of Colter's feet coming my way, moving faster than I'd ever seen him move. His ears were flopping and his tongue was hanging out and his yearling's long legs were scrambling as fast as those of a cartoon character—and I thought, Man, he really *wants* that bird.

Such was his speed, the fury of his legs churning, that he could not control his flight; he kept tripping over his chin, his body propelling itself faster, it seemed, than his legs, so that he would sometimes cartwheel; though even in his cartwheels he kept cruising along. He raced right past me—"Colter, *leave* it!" I shouted again—and he gave me this wild-eyed look that seemed to say, *What do you think I'm trying to do?*

And then right behind him came the lion, bigger than I realized a lion could be, looking like something transposed from Africa, gold as a grizzly and as large, so that at first I thought that's what it was—head as large as a basketball, and huge-shouldered—until I saw the long tail floating along behind.

It was easily twice as large as any lion I'd ever seen. I read later that occasionally males can get up to around 250 pounds, so I guess that's where this one was. At the moment, though, as the lion glided past me with a strangeness of locomotion I had never seen before—it was as if, with its long easy strides, so slow compared to the churning rpm's of Colter, the lion was floating, drawn along on some magic carpet—and as I looked down on the lion from the roadcut embankment, I could see every huge muscle working, reach-and-pull. In the shock of the moment I would have estimated the lion's weight to be about 600 pounds.

The lion was gliding right behind Colter, like some huge floating Chinese dragon in a parade, or a lazy kite string at the end of the furious dynamo of Colter. It seemed to me that at any moment the lion could have reached out its big paws and pulled down this small brown screambug rocket of a dog, but the lion seemed to be made momentarily curious by the little twitching nub of Colter's tail.

The lion passed right over my shoe tops. I could have netted him with a six-foot dip-net. There was some shadow-part way down below me and not at my core that weighed the option of being silent and still and letting this thing play itself on out and maybe, maybe, everything would somehow turn out okay, but it was just the dry shell of a consideration, having no more life to it than the husks of insect skeletons you find clinging to the sides of buildings in the early summer and braided into the nests of birds.

A boy loves his dog; a man loves his dog. "*Hey*," I said to the lion, or something like that. It was only half, or three-quarters, of a shout. "Hey, *asshole*, leave my dog alone."

The lion glanced up at me, clearly surprised, as he cruised past, but kept on gliding. Dog and lion disappeared into deep grass twenty yards away—there was a single yelp, then silence—and I could see through the tall green grass the motionless shape of that big lion.

I was afraid he had Colter down—had perhaps broken his neck with one swat—but I held out the thin hope that Colter was only in shock, and that I might somehow still be able to claim him and carry him, entrails trailing, down the mountain and into town, and get him stitched up and doctored and put back together again.

I picked up a chip of shale about the size and density of a deck of playing cards and advanced slowly toward where I could see the lion in the grass.

The lion turned and looked at me, and my first and immediate realization was to understand how easily one of these creatures could, by itself, kill a 700-pound elk. My second impression or realization was that the lion was staring at me with perhaps the purest distillation of scorn I have ever encountered. Still I advanced, yelling at the lion, trying to work up a bravery and anger that just wasn't there, and which, by that cat-scorn look, the lion *knew* wasn't there.

But I could see the lion thinking, too. I could tell that there was just enough uncertainty about things—the surprise of my appearance into the equation—for the lion to be wondering if he had not somehow blundered or been lured into a trap.

The evidence before him—a pale, trembly stick figure advancing upon him with a lone handful of dirt-rock, then pausing and staring at him—clearly did not support this hypothesis, but that was the only thing, the only thing in the world I had going for me: the uncertainty, that brief revelatory surprise, of my unplanned appearance. I could only hope that, to such an able assassin as this big lion, the lack of control in any area of his mission would be grounds for canceling his mission.

I stood there, gripping that dirt-wad, calling the lion names—hurling words at him. He did not look away from me, nor did the degree of his scorn, the intensity of it, lessen.

I saw my dog! As if my eyes were only now coming into focus, I saw Colter sitting on his haunches, knock-kneed and spraddle-legged, panting, tongue hanging out. If *scorn* was the lion's essence, in that moment I would have to say that *bewilderment* was Colter's.

I grew up in Texas, reared as a child on the Fred Gibson stories of noble dogs such as Old Yeller and Savage Sam. For long moments I entertained the belief, the longing, that under no circumstances would Colter let anything happen to me—that now that he was turned around and had the situation figured, he would in no way let that lion attack me: that he would do whatever it took to protect me. Me, the one who fed him and protected him.

The three of us formed a long flat dangerous triangle, with the lion at the apex. I called to Colter, whistled for him to slink past the lion and come stand by my side so we could make a stand, two-against-one—or, better yet, so we could get the hell out of there—but Colter only looked at me with that same panting incomprehension. He just sat there, looking all goofy, and with the heavy awareness of the responsibility of adulthood, or some other awful thing, I realized that not only was I going to have to take care of myself in this fracas, but rescue my dog, too.

It was in the end all just a little too weird for the lion. After more scowling he turned and walked off into a dense tangle of blowdown lodgepole, the bulk of his body taking up as much of that little logging road, it seemed, as a tractor-trailer, and yet after he was gone, he was really gone—vanished. When I went over to collect the panting brown sack of my dog—I had to lift him as if gathering up a limp stuffed animal—I peered into that jungle of blowdown lodgepole fully expecting to see the lion crouched in there, repositioning himself and recalculating things for a return attack.

But he was gone forever, gone from our lives anyway, though for the next couple of years stories would come from off that mountain of other hunters who'd had encounters with him. In future years enough stories would come from the same area so that it was not even like a myth, but a certainty: if you went to that spot on the map, that lion was going to fool with you. God knows what he ate: mule deer and elk, I suppose. One hunter even had several little *cubs* chase him in that area one time; surely those were somehow the lion's progeny. They were so young they were barely able to run yet, but came snarling and spitting at him anyway, little kittens. He left, too.

Another time the big lion snuck up on an elk hunter, who turned and saw the giant staring at him, crouched, at a distance of about five yards. The hunter hurled a steel hatchet at the lion and struck him—like tossing an empty aluminum can—but the lion turned and ran back off, and disappeared.

He hasn't been seen, or noted, for a couple of years now, but it's hard to believe he's not still out there. Though maybe he was already old when all that was going on, so that now, soon enough, he is motionless—that big basketball of a skull gleaming bright on a hillside somewhere, bone-sharpened teeth pearl-polished and still open as if protesting or snarling at even the rising and setting of each day's sun—the lion's long ship of bones relaxing and slipping, dissolving from its previous order—a vertebrae or two tumbling down the hill, a femur rotating awkwardly in a way it never would have in life, the lion's eerie round skull looking so somehow alien and, to our way of thinking perhaps, superior to the skulls of so many slain deer in the garden of bones on that hillside around him. . . .

But even in that repose, even in that transition from full-muscled grace to loose-boned chaos, I think a grace would return to the magnificent old lion. I think yarrow would bloom through one of the huge, perfectly round eye sockets one year. In the case of that lion's magic, anything is possible to imagine: maybe twin yarrow, from each orbital, or twin penstemon, like prayer flags in the wind. As if those bones were incapable of too long being disassociated from grace or beauty.

Perhaps for 100 years, or longer, deer on that mountainside would avoid even the location of those bones—as if believing they might yet reassemble themselves and leap up again into headlong gigantic flight.

We have no sure ways, really, of knowing anything. Our hearts and the blood of the millennia that those hearts pump know so much more than what we can read or experience in a lifetime. A mountain is like a library.

What I suspect happened with Colter and that lion—though I cannot be sure, can only guess or imagine it—is that Colter, with his excellent nose, caught wind of a grouse, and was working it, and got to it at the same time the lion was stalking it, and that the grouse flushed; and that the lion, angered—and surprised—chased Colter.

Quivery-legged, afterward, Colter and I hiked on down the mountain, glancing over our shoulders often.

III. Conflicts and Controversy:
The Politics of Predators

Looking forward to a restorative run in the woods, a jogger, mother of two young children, ties her shoes for the last time in her life. A short time later she is dead, killed by another mother, who is subsequently tracked and shot by a federal Animal Damage Control agent.

Which mother has ultimate claim to that fragrant, shadowed piece of California forest—Barbara Schoener or the mountain lion? Which is our greater responsibility as citizens: to ensure absolute protection for our families, pets, livestock, and livelihoods, or to protect and preserve the last remaining major predator to prowl among us? The mountain lion has swallowed these questions and given them form; it has loaned its sleek shape to abstract issues of wildlands and species protection and carries our ambivalence grumbling in its belly.

Generally speaking, where they still exist in the West mountain lions aren't threatened or endangered. Without the legal restrictions and emotional clarity that guide our decisions regarding endangered species, we are obliged to chart a more murky course in our dealings with *Felis concolor*. Do we control lion numbers or do we let nature take its own course? If we do control them, how? Or more precisely, who? Government agents? Do we allow people to hunt mountain lions? With dogs? If a mountain lion wanders down a suburban street, should it be shot or relocated? What if it wanders into a schoolyard?

Unless you own a ranch, a construction company, or a logging operation, wolves, grizzly bears, snail darters, and spotted owls pose little threat or inconvenience. But mountain lions still have the potential to affect the daily lives of a significant number of people. We've labored for generations to make life safe and convenient, but now there are mountain lions in the neighborhood. As a modern society we say we value the wholeness of ecosystems, but that's been from an uncontested view at the top of the food chain. Forcing us to make room there, the mountain lion tests our commitment. The presence of predators requires compromise. We might be asked to confine pets, change development and husbandry practices, and hike in pairs—or not hike at all on certain trails at certain times. If we accept predators among us, life will no longer be at the exclusive convenience of our own species.

Compromise and tolerance are relatively recent concepts in our approach to predators. As early as 1695, South Carolina lawmakers passed the Act for Destroying Beasts of Prey, and government policies advocating blanket eradication of predators survived well into the twentieth century. Grizzly bears and wolves were effectively eliminated from all but a shred of their original range, but mountain lions still stalk the margins of our urban sprawl and the edges of our environmental ethos.

The transition from rural to urban society has been accompanied by a distinct shift in attitude toward predators. The last state program to pay a bounty for dead cougars (in Arizona) ended in 1970. Few of us raise chickens or lambs or calves in order to feed ourselves or to make a living, and the majority of predators have already been "conquered," so in our comfort and detachment we have come to view predators as somewhat abstract symbols of an intact and functioning ecosystem, rather than as a personal threat. That is, until a mountain lion stalks our children or eats our pets. In California, after cougars had attacked eight people and killed two, voters still narrowly defeated a proposal to open a cougar hunting season.

Even though a hunting season was shot down, about 100 lions are killed in California at public request each year for real and perceived threats to people and livestock. In addition to the mountain lions killed throughout the West in such state-managed control efforts, about 260 lions are killed each year by federal Wildlife Services (formerly Animal Damage Control) agents employed to reduce predation on livestock and to destroy animals that have become habituated to humans.

In spite of current control programs and past anti-cougar campaigns, the mountain lion is doing surprisingly well in many areas of the West. Biologists estimate that 10,000 to 50,000 cougars roam through Montana, Idaho, Wyoming, Colorado, Utah, Nevada, Arizona, New Mexico, Texas, Washington, Oregon, and California. (There are no verified mountain lion populations left in the eastern two-thirds of the United States, except for the thirty to fifty Florida panthers facing down their extinction in the Everglades.)

Ironically, the policies of classifying cougars as game animals and establishing hunting seasons are credited with saving western cougar populations. The cats had been considered varmints until the early 1960s, making it legal to kill or harass them at any time, but game animal status carried the protection of restricted seasons and bag limits. Today, cougars are hunted under regulated seasons in all western states except Texas and California. In Texas, mountain lions may be hunted at any time of year, and in California, mountain lion hunting has been essentially banned since the early 1970s.

Although Oregon and Washington both allow mountain lion hunting, voters in those states passed initiatives outlawing the use of dogs in the hunting of cats. In all other western states, hound hunting is legal. In the simplest quantifiable terms, hunting is the greatest cause of cougar mortality, with about 2,600 cats killed legally each year. Researchers, managers, hunters, and preservationists debate the effect of hunting on overall populations, and ponder the ethics of hunting mountain lions. But many agree that habitat loss is probably the most serious long-term threat to the lion's future.

Historically, we have declined to share our living space with wildlife any more troublesome than certain birds and squirrels. Not only have we secured our perimeters against bears and mountain lions, but we have also ejected skunks, porcupines, moles, mice, and bats. The conflict over territory was less urgent when space wasn't at such a premium—when wilderness was unbroken by roads, towns, and truck stop casinos; and before the lion's traditional territory had been fragmented into isolated patches of "habitat," a term now adopted by zoos for their animal enclosures. The conflict was less urgent when people ventured "out" into wildlands, and the rare itinerant mountain lion came "in" to town. But galloping suburban development and the growing ranks of outdoor enthusiasts have ruptured that boundary.

What now? What management strategies will provide a balance between safety and stewardship? How can we reconcile legitimate traditions of hunting and ranching with the compelling desire to protect our beautiful American lion and the dwindling wilderness it has come to represent?

In the following pages, people of varying perspectives—including an animal rights activist, a hunter, a mountain lion researcher, a rancher, and the ranger who helped recover Barbara Schoener's body—explore their relationships to the mountain lion and to the places lions inhabit in their physical and emotional landscapes. Whether you're more likely to collect signatures for ballot initiatives or to run hounds, you're invited to join this hunt for understanding through its interesting tangle of conflicts.

A Natural Death

by Jordan Fisher-Smith

I met a Californian who would
Talk California—a state so blessed
He said, in climate, none had ever died there
A natural death. . . .

—ROBERT FROST, from "New Hampshire"

There is a sort of memory that does not refer to a particular day; yet it is not without precision, and accumulates from just being in a place for a period of years. Each time the American River floods big and brown with snowmelt and rain, I remember better the way huge drift logs turn ponderous circles in eddies, and where the river is carrying away land at the outside of turns, and where it builds beaches at the inside of them. Later, on warm spring days after the rains are past, I remember how little pink trumpets of bilobed clarkia and yellow daisies of eriophyllum float, as if mounted on some transparent medium a certain number of inches, according to their species, above the steep hillsides; and how for ten or twelve feet above that colorful surface there is a layer of air that hums and sparkles in the sun, composed substantially of insects seeking nectar.

I know where there is a tiny patch of a St. John's wort, called gold-wire for the shine of its filamentous stamens, tucked up under the chemise brush at the top of a red clay bank on a turn in the old Doc Gordon Road above Lake Clementine; it took me ten years to find it. Sometimes in summer one of the thunderstorms that boil up against the Sierra Nevada every afternoon reaches out as far as the foothills to the west, and a sweet damp smell rises from the dust just before the first drops of rain. The novelty of rain is one of the few things I like about hot summers in the canyons, a season I mostly detest. To be fair, however, the things I dislike about that time—the merciless sun old forests would have shaded me from; the dust on my face, my uniform, and rescue equipment from the dirt roads I travel, which hemorrhage clouds of soil behind every car; the spiny star thistle that gets to flesh through thick jeans, the wild oats that lodge in your socks, and the other disagreeable European annuals that overwhelm the perennial meadows of the low Sierra—are the marks of 140 years of bad treatment of this land since the California gold rush. So in the eleven summers I have worked as a ranger in these canyons I have tried to forgive their bad manners and prickliness, for these are the inevitable outcomes of servitude in land as in people.

Aside from the memorization of these things that repeat themselves annually until the idle gaze comprehends them, I am prone to a natural indolence of memory, and I am content to let hours of work steal by without straining to save the details for posterity; I am a poor keeper of patrol logs; better get someone else to do it. For anyone who suffers from such an undisciplined dreaminess as I do, the quieter days are as seamless and unaccountable as water slipping by in the river, until time is apprehended by the duty to record something, such as the report, late in the day on April 23, 1994, that a woman named Barbara Schoener was missing up the Middle Fork.

The only thing I recall about the earlier part of that day, before the call came in, is an observation I made of the weather. At midmorning, I steered my green Jeep off Route 49 into the entrance of the gray gravel road up the south bank of the Middle Fork, and drove to the old limestone quarry. I turned off the engine and looked up the river, in the direction Barbara Schoener was, a few miles east, although I did not know it. The sky was deep blue around harmless-looking puffy white clouds. The air was clear and cool. The sun was warm on my left elbow out the open window. The riffles in the river whispered and sparkled in the eastern light.

Weather is a deciding factor in any search, in the survival of the lost or injured or, if there is nothing left to do for them, in the difficulty and discomfort of recovering the remains. In this case, morning made a false promise. By nightfall, the clouds gathered into a dark sheet and set upon the searchers, soaking them to the skin with a cold, steady rain.

———

What you do to investigate an accidental death is a little like being a theater director. Arriving late, you find the actors and props spread around the stage in disordered repose. In your mind's eye, you send them back to first positions, marked in the theater with little pieces of tape on the stage, and in the woods by footprints, the victim's personal effects, and an unclaimed automobile at the trailhead. Then you set them in motion on the stage of your imagination, over and over, until you get it right.

Later, when the report is written and the usefulness of thinking about it is long over, it's hard to forget this omniscient vision you've made of the victim's fated progress toward a bad end you know about, and they don't.

So it is that I see Barbara Schoener driving north from her home in Placerville. California poppies unfurl their glossy orange petals into the morning light between clumps of blue lupine on the roadcuts along State Route 49, two lanes of winding asphalt and a double center line of yellow paint twisting along the front of the Sierra, connecting the string of little white-painted wood and brick mining towns with corrugated steel roofs. About half an hour north she comes to the town of Cool, a group of plywood false-fronts like a western movie set and a county fire station set down in the middle of rolling pasture punctuated by stately blue oaks. She turns east at the only inter-section in town onto State 193, past the dirt turnout on the east side of the junction where scruffy men from the hills sell fire-wood out of beat-up trucks, advertising their loads with spray-painted signs on scraps of plywood.

Just east of there, Barbara Schoener passes the main gate of a residential development along the south rim of the Middle Fork canyon, expectantly named Auburn Lake Trails—expectantly, because if a proposed dam isn't built in the canyon below it, there may never be a lake anywhere near Auburn Lake Trails. Auburn Lake Trails is one of those gated communities that have turned old ranches into recreational landscapes, with remnants of barbed wire fences on split cedar posts going to rust and rot between big plywood houses on an aimless road network.

There are two more gates into Auburn Lake Trails in the next few miles east on 193, electric ones that can be opened by magnetic security cards the residents carry. Barbara Schoener parks her car outside the second, across a perfectly paved road from the development's water treatment plant.

The woman who gets out of the car is forty years of age,

athletic, attractive, the mother of two children, with shoulder-length reddish brown hair. She wears a pair of blue nylon shorts, a cranberry sleeveless T-shirt, running shoes, and a hat and cotton gloves against the morning chill. She locks the car and puts the key in a little pouch attached to one of her shoes. Carrying an apple and a water bottle, she leaves the road, running down the trail into the neighboring state park.

At first she follows an old dirt road, grown over on either side by Scotch broom and narrowed to a single track. Horses and rain have worn a rut into the center of the remaining path; she places her feet with care. The road descends quickly into a Douglas fir forest so that only a few feet from her car she is quite alone. Then the trail abandons the road, traversing the canyonside on contour, following the folds of creeks. Presently, it comes out onto an open ridge. Far below, the river is spread out in a slow bend, silver against its gray gravel bed. She pauses to look, to have something to eat, breathing deeply of the air in which something bright, dust, a bit of pollen, catches the light over the void. Ahead, entering the forest again, the path bends left into the manzanita.

—

At five o'clock in the evening, as I drove north on 49 toward the ranger station to go home, the radio dispatcher called me. She turned me around, back across the North Fork and the El Dorado County line, to meet with the sheriff's deputies about a search in progress.

The missing woman's sedan was cordoned off with yellow crime scene ribbon. The sheriff's search and rescue volunteers in orange shirts hustled around a mobile communications van. The wind was picking up. I got my jacket out of the back of the Jeep and shook hands with the officer in charge.

He said that when Barbara Schoener had failed to return as expected from a run, her husband reported the matter to the sheriff. Her husband knew that she liked to run on this trail, and her car was located at the trailhead. She was probably equipped only with light clothing. The deputy and I agreed that I would drive up the Quarry Road at the bottom of the canyon. There was a chance I would find her down along the river; when people get lost they often head downhill until they get to something they can't cross.

It was dusk by the time I got back down to the rusty gate into the Quarry Road. I let myself in and idled slowly east with the river on my left, watching the road shoulder on my right—we say "cutting it for sign"—for the lost woman's footprints. It started to drizzle and I turned on the wipers. About two miles farther on at Brown's Bar, the road gets narrow and bad. The tires began to slip and throw bits of red clay up onto the hood. It got dark.

This was the reassuringly familiar landscape of my nights, the interior of a Jeep, an exoskeleton of green humming steel, inside which I was surrounded by heated air and safe from most things, animals and weather, and compared to a foot traveler, freed from the tyranny of distance. All businesslike: the tan upholstery of my seat, the lower right of its back torn from the constant abrasion of the grips of my pistol, the flashlight wedged between my right thigh and the radio console between the seats, and from this the cheerful blinking lights and a low chorus of calm voices from all the rural counties around me, the men and women, police officers, rangers, paramedics, firefighters, the pilots of medical evacuation helicopters, who come and go all night cleaning up scenes of chaos and imposing upon them the appearance of order that society requires in order to sleep well.

I turned on the light bar so that if Barbara Schoener could move and was somewhere above me she would see me coming from a long way off, and would have time to get down to the road. Spokes of red and blue light circled me across the slopes of the canyon and the raindrops. I turned on all the spotlights, training them in different directions so I could watch for her, as I imagined it, waving urgently in the darkness. I reached down to my right, punched up the loudspeaker, and pulled the mike off the dashboard.

"If you can walk, come down to my lights here on the road! Come to my lights!" I called over and over.

And as I did so, it dawned on me that Barbara Schoener was gone. It was just a feeling, after all those years of searches, that I was talking to myself, that there was no one to hear me when I called to her. But still I called again and again, sending my amplified voice washing out over the cold boiling surface of the river, surrounding the dark trees and thickets of manzanita, filling up secret hollows.

Beyond Main Bar Creek, the Quarry Road becomes two Jeep tracks across the sand and round gray cobbles of the gravel bars. I stopped to put the Jeep in low range and got out into the rain to listen and have a look around. Across the side of the canyon, several hundred feet above me to the south and east through the mist of rain, I saw the twinkling flashlights of other searchers. I got back in, and bounced and scraped upstream across the boulders to the end of the road, watching the pools of my spotlights move across the feathery limbs of fir trees up the side of the canyon and straining to listen, through the roar of the rapids and the whine of the gearbox, for a cry in the darkness.

—

The American River figured prominently in California's environmental history long before Barbara Schoener became the first Californian in the twentieth century to be killed and eaten by a mountain lion, a species that at one point not too many years ago looked as if it might eventually disappear from California.

In 1848, the news that gold had been discovered on the river's South Fork set off the 1849 gold rush. What followed was 140-odd years of alterations to the landscape. Forests of huge ponderosa pines and Douglas fir in the canyons were soon cut over for the lumber to build towns like Auburn and Placerville; for

water flumes, train trestles, and timbers for the mines; for fuel-
wood and for charcoal for lime kilns. Placer and hydraulic miners poured so much silt and gravel down these Sierra rivers that
San Francisco Bay, where these rivers reach the sea, was said to
have lost a quarter of its size over the following years. Miners
and settlers went about exterminating native occupants, game,
and predators of this territory with biblical authority, and they
worshiped in churches and drank in bars and got rich in assay
offices thrown up out of perfectly knot-free and fine-grained
boards from ancient trees, the likes of which we will not see
coming out of Sierra forests again, not in this lifetime anyway.

By my boyhood thirty-five years ago most of the mines had
shut down after a disastrous fall in the price of gold, and the land
was yoked by cattle ranches or lay fallow in speculation. Then in
1964 another form of plunder was planned for these canyons;
they were to be drowned under a huge reservoir as part of the
grand plumbing project that supplies agriculture and urban
development in the thirsty southern half of the state. The dam,
to be built by the federal government's Bureau of Reclamation,
was to be 700 feet high, spanning 4,150 feet across the American's
North Fork downstream of its confluence with the Middle Fork,
creating a deep and narrow Y-shaped reservoir that would flood
about forty-eight miles of the river.

But by the time work on the dam got under way in the early
1970s, the public's wide-eyed confidence in acts of grand-scale engi-
neering hubris had given way to concern about the destruction of
the American River landscape, and, downstream in the flood-
prone Sacramento plain, outright fear, after the revelation that
there were earthquake faults in the rocks beneath the dam site.

By the time the political outcomes of this new awareness hit
the Bureau's budget, the agency had already acquired the land,
moved the inhabitants off of it, and let a contract with the
California State Parks to operate the proposed lake as a public
recreation area. Park rangers moved in. In 1986 I joined them.

Management of the canyons in those years consisted mostly of meandering, improvising, and waiting for news on the fate of the dam. The only official plan we had for the new state park wasn't much help; it was all about a lake that didn't exist.

However, if uncertainty about the changing fortunes of the Auburn Dam created in State Park and Bureau of Reclamation offices an atmosphere lacking in the sense of permanence that people who manage public lands ought to feel, the land itself lacked the capacity to equivocate in the face of this uncertainty. In the nearly thirty years since the government acquired the American River country from its previous owners, the place had begun to go seriously wild again and to repopulate itself with the things whose habit it had been to live there before the Euro-American conquest. And no one at State Parks or the Bureau was, or is now, studying this process.

—

Meanwhile, if the numbers of some wildlife had crept back up under a regimen of benign neglect, human population around the American River canyons had soared.

In 1970 there were just over twenty million people in California. The population of El Dorado County, where Barbara Schoener lived and died, was around 44,000. That was not much, considering that El Dorado County at 1,711 square miles is just a little smaller than the state of Delaware.

By 1994 California's population had grown to 31.4 million, a little over one and a half times what it was in 1970. In the same period El Dorado County's population had more than tripled to 146,400 souls. Most of them settled in the lower-elevation western part of the county around the American River canyons, where they would be spared the serious snow-shoveling common in the high country and the commute to jobs in the greater Sacramento area was reasonable. In the late 1980s these counties along the foothill front of the Sierra Nevada were among the fastest-growing in the state.

Today, if you take a drive up these rural roads in the foothills and allow yourself to wander, you will end up on dusty roads off of other unmarked roads, off of other roads. And at the end of each of them sits a relatively new house with no economic relationship, such as a ranch house or a miner's cabin would have, to the land around it. Everything that gets up there, from the next quart of milk to the next stick of lumber for a fence, gets there in an automobile, a pickup truck, or a sport-utility vehicle. It is a way of life unprecedented in history, and one so freshly arrived in these hills that some of its attractiveness may be residual from the activities of previous occupants, such as the vigilant extermination of predators carried out by cattlemen and by the government in their stead. So for a few years, hikers and runners from the new housing developments in the western Sierra have been safer in these woods than anyone might have been there for thousands of years.

———

On the morning of April 24, the second day of the search, four young men, long-distance runners and acquaintances of Barbara Schoener's, went out to look for her. At about 7:15 A.M., they found her water bottle along the Ball Bearing Trail. Nearby, they saw signs of a struggle in the duff down the side of the mountain below the trail. They followed these marks just far enough to see Barbara Schoener's feet sticking out of a pile of sticks and forest litter farther into the draw. They ran back to the trailhead and reported that they had found her, dead.

I made arrangements with my contact at the Sheriff-Coroner's office to meet for a death scene investigation later in the day, upon the arrival of a forensics specialist from the Department of Justice. Could be a homicide, he said. She's covered up, as if to conceal her body.

Around four, I drove through Auburn Lake Trails to the edge of the canyon. There I met the Sheriff-Coroner's deputies and the Department of Justice forensic technician, a cheerful woman named Faye in a blue jumpsuit. Hands were shaken, introductions made, outcomes of other recent investigations asked about as we loaded cameras, equipment, and body bag into backpacks.

We started up the trail at the opposite end from where Barbara Schoener had entered—it was the shorter way in to where she was—only about a half-mile at the most from the nearest house, a conventional two-car garage place on a neat asphalt cul-de-sac that sits incongruously in the middle of the grass and trees as if it had dropped from the sky. The switchbacks we walked up in the first 100 feet of the trail were brand-new work. No one would have been likely to have been killed by an animal on this trail thirty years ago. The trail hadn't existed then, and neither had the road to the trailhead, nor the house.

We came to a place where the path traversed along a hillside, falling off steeply to the left in the shade of oaks and firs. Some horses with orange search and rescue stuff hanging from their saddles stood in the trail, tied up to trees. Just beyond them, we ducked under a barrier of police crime scene ribbon. Three sheriff's search and rescue volunteers in orange shirts, ballcaps, and cowboy belt buckles were setting up fixed ropes down the steep hillside to assist us in getting the body out. They spoke to each other in low, funereal tones. I nodded a greeting to each of them as we passed, and they nodded back grimly.

About 300 feet farther, the trail curved out from under the trees onto a rocky ridge surrounded by manzanita bushes that provided cover close to the path for anything that would want it. One of the Sheriff-Coroner's deputies pointed out a divot of moss, loosened from the bank above the trail, below the manzanita.

As we reconstructed it, the cougar had been sitting in the brush, hungry maybe, perhaps lying in wait for the next animal to come along the path. That happened to be a runner, a woman. The animal sprang down the bank, leaving the divot as it launched. It hit the woman from above and behind. She staggered off the downhill side of the trail into the softer duff, where her feet left two unmistakably deep impressions; she was heavy with the weight of both of them, struggling to remain standing. She went down against a fallen fir sapling which lay across the slope below the trail. There had been a struggle; branches were broken off the dead tree, and there was a dark stain on the soil which smelled a way you don't forget. She stood up again and staggered downhill over the tree. There were a few more footprints in the duff. Just below and to the left of these, at the base of a Douglas fir sapling, I found one of Barbara Schoener's cotton gloves soaked red with blood, and a Red Delicious apple with her dainty bites around its circumference.

From where these things lay there were scuffs down to the bottom of the steeper portion of the slope below the trail, maybe a hundred feet. There the dragging started, leaving a furrow in the ferns just as wide as a small woman's body for another hundred feet to where we found her.

Once, years before, as a boy hiking alone in the redwoods near my home, I had stumbled on a mountain lion kill, a deer, dragged into a cool canyon and covered with sticks so the cat could come back later to eat more. Nothing was scattered around; there was a kind of fastidiousness to it.

—

The legislative history of cougars in California reflects the change in attitudes toward predators with the growth of an environmental ethic in the 1960s and 1970s, and the changing composition of the state's demographics from rural-agricultural to primarily urban-suburban. Increased protection for mountain lions would probably not have occurred had the legislature continued to reflect the wishes of any sizable constituency who had their next mortgage payment tied up in a flock of stupid and defenseless sheep standing around at night in a remote mountain meadow.

When I was a boy, if you saw a lion you could shoot it and collect the bounty from the state government: $50 for a female and

$60 for a male, and this was sometimes enhanced by counties.

There may have been only 2,000 to 2,500 lions left in the state in midcentury. After 1963 the bounty was removed and the cougar classified as a nongame mammal. In 1969 California reclassified the mountain lion as a game mammal, and for two years permits were issued to hunt them for sport. In 1972, as younger wildlife managers brought to their work an appreciation for the role of predators in healthy ecosystems and concern grew for the shrinking populations of cougars, lions were protected entirely from hunting, except as necessary to protect lives and property. The shape of this protection has not changed appreciably to the present day. It has always been possible to get a depredation permit to kill one or several lions if they threatened people or livestock. The lions are generally exterminated by trappers from the U.S. Department of Agriculture's Animal Damage Control program, by the rancher who requested the permit, or by a game warden from Fish and Game. In 1995, 131 lion depredation permits were issued in California, and 118 lions were killed.

In 1990, California's voters passed a law known as Proposition 117, confirming their preference that the cougar not be hunted. The new law also created a habitat conservation fund for the purchase of wildland inhabited by cougars. Since much, maybe most, of California is cougar habitat, this provided for the purchase of parks and reserves that in practice also protect all kinds of other wildlife that happen to cohabit them.

But critics of the cougar's protected status say that under the current regime, the state Department of Fish and Game has not been allowed to manage the overall population growth of cougars by opening a hunting season. They say the cougar population is expanding, out of control. They point out, and most biologists agree with this point, that cougars' pattern of habitat utilization involves the ejection of younger animals from more desirably remote country already occupied by dominant older animals, into marginal areas along the suburban edges of wild-lands. This, say the lion's critics, will increasingly bring young cougars into contact with people in the suburbs, and before long they will be experimenting with stealing children from their bicycles. That's hysteria, say the cougar's supporters.

—

Our retribution for the death of Barbara Schoener was swift. When I returned at seven in the evening from picking up the body, I notified the Department of Fish and Game's dispatch office. They notified the U.S. Department of Agriculture's Animal Damage Control Service trappers. The following morning I returned to the scene of the kill with two trappers and three Fish and Game wardens to begin the hunt.

Lions are hunted either by baiting them in with a captive farm animal, or by running them down with specially trained dogs. In the latter process, a houndsman will drive a rural road with the lead dog standing on top of his specially built truck until the dog, crossing a scent on the wind, gives voice. Then the trapper lets the rest of the dogs out of their cages in the back of the truck, and puts them on the chase. A single dog is no match for a lion, but lions are scared by a pack of them. A lion will climb to a high spot, a cliff or a tree, and the dogs will keep the animal there and howl at it until the hunter catches up. Then it's like killing fish in a barrel, if you have a rifle or pistol.

That's basically how it was done. After eight days of tracking and dog work, the ADC hunters picked up the lion's scent again, when the lion came back to the scene of the kill, maybe to get more meat. The chase was short, and the cougar was soon treed and shot a half-mile away, just the other side of Main Bar Creek.

The dead lion was an eighty-three-pound female. Barbara Schoener outweighed her by about twenty pounds. The lion's udders were full, which meant she had a cub. Over the next couple of days the trappers went back out and found a kitten, which was displayed for the news cameras and then turned over to a zoo.

On the twelfth of May, I sat in a lecture theater at the University of California Medical School at Davis among newspaper and television reporters, state officials, and representatives from animal rights organizations. A procession of experts in forensic fields took the stage and described how they had identified the dead cougar as the one that had killed Barbara Schoener. A forensic odontologist had matched the animal's teeth with impressions they had left in Barbara Schoener's crushed skull. Experts in DNA typing had swabbed the folds of skin that the animal's claws retract into (as a housecat's do) and located human DNA—and not just any human DNA, but the same type as Barbara Schoener's. They had killed the right lion.

It did not stop there.

During that same year, at another California state park hundreds of miles to the south, in San Diego County just north of the Mexican border, there had been a series of disturbing incidents and close calls between lions and hikers. One ought to be cautious about drawing conclusions, yet there are some resemblances between the places: like Auburn, Cuyamaca Rancho State Park had for many years been working land, a cattle ranch, and had later been deeded to the State Park System. San Diego County, like El Dorado County, had seen a massive invasion of its brushy hills by housing tracts.

At Cuyamaca on December 10, 1994, eight months after California's first killing of a human being by a lion in over a hundred years, another woman, fifty-six-year-old Marie Kenna, was dragged off a fire road and mauled to death by a cougar while hiking alone near a popular campground. There has not been another such death in California in three years, at this writing.

Including the 1994 fatalities of Barbara Schoener and Marie Kenna, there have been only ten attacks by cougars on people in California since 1890. Two of the attacks involved two victims each. Eight of the attacks have occurred since 1986. Including the 1890 incident, three of these people died from their injuries.

Two more in 1909 died from rabies they contracted from a lion that attacked but did not kill them.

The roughly 220,000 human beings who die in California each year do so primarily of disease. Those who die violently do so primarily as the result of the actions of other human beings or their own actions, not the actions of animals. In 1994, the unheard-of year in which two women in the state were killed by mountain lions, there were 3,821 homicides and 4,212 traffic fatalities in California.

After the 1994 kills, an angry "eye for an eye" sentiment prevailed among conservatives in the state legislature. Several bills were introduced to reinstate sport hunting of lions with dogs in California, supported and sponsored by hunters' clubs. An initiative statute was prepared for the March 1996 primary election to repeal the protection mountain lions had enjoyed from hunting, and assign Fish and Game to manage and control the cougar population. It was roundly defeated by the voters. Urban and suburban people in California like their wildlife. Most of them have never even seen a lion and many would like to see one, under the right circumstances.

I have seen only two cougars in my life, eighteen years of which I have spent working as a ranger in lion habitat. One of them ran across the Foresthill Road in front of my Jeep about two miles as the crow flies from where Barbara Schoener was killed. I have patrolled these roads in Jeeps, the trails on foot, and the rivers in boats for another six years now without seeing one again. I wager they have seen me, often. That's what mountain lions do for a living: they remain concealed.

How many lions are there in California? No one really knows. Because they are hard to see, cougars are hard to count. And because they are hard to count, it would be hard to manage their populations in any precise way. The last official study of the state's lion population, in 1988, resulted in an estimate of 5,100. The Department of Fish and Game's current official estimate is

4,000 to 6,000 lions. They exist in the spaces between thirty-two million people and countless domestic animals, who are actively invading the wilds.

—

When I started rangering I used to think I was there to do something, to save something. I do little things, I save some things, but I am beginning to think I am there to witness: the light, the green, the sound of water, rocks falling off a mountain, the glint of animal eyes in the brush along the roads at night, the good and bad things that happen on the edge between people and open country.

What memory distills from ten years of witnessing is a glimpse of the general direction of things: the return of a cool ponderosa pine and Douglas fir forest, pushing up through live oaks and black oaks; the profusion of wildflowers in the meadows after cattle were removed; and the growing frequency of sightings and tracks of mountain lion and black bear. After a century and a half of condemnation to usefulness, there is a great longing back toward wildness in these canyons, and they go that way with an energy like continental drift, like roots heaving pavement. It is desire; it is the force behind everything that happens without human permission or design. It is present in the heartbeats of tiny birds that roost in trees on nights when we would quickly perish from exposure, were it not for our houses and warm clothes. When this energy brings the missing parts back to a place, it is uneven, unpredictable; and, as in the case of Barbara Schoener, it can be dangerous.

I will never forget how she looked, surrounded by the way things are at that time of the spring on a north-facing slope: young Douglas firs, green ferns and moss in the dappled light.

At five o'clock in the evening on April 24, as the low sun turned the tops of the conifers orange above us, four of us walked down into the forest below the Ball Bearing Trail and knelt in the sword ferns around the neat mound of duff and sticks that covered the body, except for the top of the scalp and the neatly tied running shoes. The evidence technician and I began to remove the pile of twigs one at a time, inspecting them for animal or human hairs, which we collected by touching them with pieces of adhesive tape and then sticking the tape down onto white evidence cards. The two Sheriff-Coroner's deputies presided, taking notes, labeling, and packaging the evidence in brown paper shopping bags.

The little glade seemed strangely peaceful.

When we finished, for a moment, the glistening internal wilds of spine, ribs, and intercostal muscles looked like food, like the inside of some deer. We gently rolled her over. Her face was gone. From below us through the deepening shadow of the forest, the roar of the rapids along the Middle Fork rose and fell on a breeze between us and the river. That sound is behind everything I remember in those canyons, like the sound, or a name I know but cannot pronounce, of some larger turning of things into other things. We photographed her, and then we put her in a body bag and bore her back up the hill.

Eat of This Flesh

by David Quammen

It's an experimental procedure, so far as I'm concerned. The work will take about thirty minutes. Wearing a gray short-sleeve scrub shirt, Dr. Don Thomas performs briskly, with an experienced physician's offhand precision. His knife is sharp, his preparation has been judicious, and for a while there will be no sign of blood. First he opens himself a beer and passes one to me.

Then he sprinkles a few drops of sesame oil onto the wok and spreads that with his fingers, like liniment rubbed into an achy shoulder. The wok's rusty iron takes a dark sheen. He dices the scallions. He dices the celery, the water chestnuts. The bok choy he dismantles leaf by leaf, chopping each leaf into largish patches. There's no vehement whapping staccato of knife blade against cutting board, since Dr. Thomas isn't one of those operatic chefs, and we talk ramblingly about other things as he works. Meanwhile, mesmerized by his cookery, hungry but ambivalent, I watch every move. He cuts open the red bell pepper, also the green one, and slices them into julienne strips. He pauses for a sip of his beer. He tosses some sesame oil into a skillet on the other burner—a more generous dosage, I notice, than granted to the wok. He cranks up the heat. And now, with a quick move to the fridge, he brings out the meat: two bowls full of mountain lion.

It's prime cut, the stuff that a hunter would call backstrap. A nonhunting carnivore would know it as part of a T-bone. To an on-duty biologist, paraspinal muscle of *Felis concolor* in the postmortem state. One bowl contains thin-cut medallions. The other, cubes. The lion flesh is pinkish and unappetizing—but not notably less appetizing than raw pork.

The medallions land sizzling in the hot wok. The cubes go into the skillet, where Thomas gives them a fast browning and then sets them to a slow, thorough simmer. (Trichinosis, he tells me, is a hazard of undercooked lion. But that doesn't mean that the meat has to be hot-fried until it's as sturdy as Vibram.) The air fills with aroma, and not just the aroma of sesame. The bok choy, the scallions, the peppers, the other items go tumbling into one dish or the other. A splash of soy to the skillet, a splash of oyster sauce to the wok. A can of pineapple chunks stands opened and ready. A jar of black bean sauce makes its appearance. While my ambivalence holds at an intermediate level, my hunger ascends toward the ceiling on Cantonese steam.

Already I can tell that Don Thomas, a bright and bristly man with whom I've had a contentious acquaintance, has proved the first of his points: whatever arguments might be made against the hunting of mountain lions, inedibility isn't one of them.

—

Personal ethics involves the drawing of lines: I will go as far as this boundary, but I will not go beyond. I will defend myself against physical menace, but only pacifically. I will fight if attacked, but I won't kill. I will kill if my family is threatened, but I won't aggress. I will squash an earwig in the kitchen but not a beetle in the yard. I will eat plants but not animals. I will eat tuna but not dolphin. I will eat goat but not pig. Fruit but not vegetables. I'm a Jainist; I will harm no living thing—except when I breathe or walk down the street, and then only unintentionally. There's a fuddling welter of such crisscrossing strictures, each observed by its own faction of conscientious people. We all draw our lines in different places, at different angles, and for different reasons, each draft reflecting a mix of individualized factors that include sensibility, emotion, experience, and taste (in both the broad and the narrow senses of that word), as well as sheer righteous logic. Moral philosophy, unfortunately, is not one of the mathematical sciences.

I will let the butcher do all of my killing. I will destroy habitat, but not animals. I will eat stir-fried shrimp, stir-fried beef, even stir-fried elk, but not stir-fried lion. Huh? Not every crisp line represents a triumph of ethical clarity.

Don Thomas draws lines of his own. He will hunt, but not with a gun. He uses a bow. He will kill lions and bears, which are thought of by most hunters as trophy-only game, but he refuses to waste the meat. He will focus his hunting efforts toward trophy-size animals and hang trophy-size heads on his walls, but he declines to enter them in the competitive record book. And even within the small domain of bow hunting, he draws a line: traditional weaponry only. Thomas eschews the fancy compound bows—with their pulleys, their lighted sight pins, their release aids, their overdraws, their lightweight arrows, and their other high-tech gimmicks—that have made bow hunting vastly easier and more lethal during the past twenty years. Bow hunting is *supposed* to be much harder than hunting with a rifle, Thomas says. That's a large part of the point. He uses only long bows and recurves, gracefully simple weapons built by craftsmen he knows from materials such as maple and elm and glue. This is a preference and a scruple, he admits, of which the significance is purely personal.

When hunting, Thomas takes only short-range shots (no more than thirty yards, generally much less) that demand fastidious stalking and raise the likelihood that a hit will be a kill. In autumn he hunts deer, elk, and antelope. Sometimes he goes to Alaska and kills a caribou or a moose. In the depth of winter, with deer season closed and snow piling up in the coulees, he hunts mountain lion. Because lion hunting is impracticable without dogs, he has trained up a good hound. Although he trees a few lions each year and has been at it for almost a decade, he has killed only one. The taxidermied hide of that lion stands in his living room, a handsome but stiff effigy of a splendid animal. Its flesh has long since been eaten. At some point in the future, he says, maybe he'll kill another. In the meantime he will continue enjoying the hunt as a process not dependent on its result. All of these facts are fundamental to Don Thomas's sense of identity. And there's another fact, somewhat more ancillary: he earns his living by practicing medicine in a small town in central Montana.

Thomas is a complicated fellow, not easily captured within categories. As an undergraduate at Berkeley in the late sixties, he was in tune with the zeitgeist, wearing his hair long, protesting the war. Asked if he was a "hippie freak" in those years, he laughs mildly and answers yes. He missed Woodstock but went to Altamont, tasting the sour dregs of the era. He had majored in English at Berkeley and felt a hankering to write, but then he shifted toward medicine instead. Medicine was a family tradition—his grandfather had been a country doctor in Texas, his father was a distinguished medical researcher who would eventually win a Nobel Prize. After medical school, Don spent two years with the Indian Health Service on a reservation in central

Montana, where he felt the reawakening of an old childhood interest: bow hunting. Some of his hunting pals at that time were Indians, but unlike him they felt no inclination toward bow and arrows. He killed his first deer with a bow in 1977, not long after having settled in the town where he lives today.

Also in 1977, he got his first glimpse of the print of a mountain lion. "And that was almost like seeing an abominable snowman track," he recalls. The species was so rare—or at least it seemed to be, after decades of persecution—that many ranchers and most town folk lived their lives without ever seeing one.

During the early 1980s, Thomas was in Alaska, doing some medicine, some commercial fishing, some bush flying, and a lot of bow hunting. He returned to Montana in 1986 and had another life-changing experience. Hiking in the mountains that summer, as he recounts, "I came over a rise and saw a mountain lion, about fifty yards in front of me." It was his first sight of *Felis concolor* in the wild. He was downwind, the lion didn't notice him, and for half an hour he watched the animal working its way along a rimrock. "That was one of the most powerful experiences I've ever had with an animal in the outdoors." This was not Yellowstone, or a zoo—this was practically his backyard.

"Something clicked," Thomas says. "I knew that I somehow had to interact with these animals."

His interaction took the form of hunting, and though that leap of logic may seem perverse and paradoxical, I can't dismiss it as nonsense, because I remember a similar weird logic in my own feelings about trout. When I first became familiar with wild trout in mountain rivers, they seemed so exquisitely gorgeous, so thrilling, so magically animate, that I wanted to interact with them somehow. I wanted to participate in the darting, lambent dynamics of their lives within their environment. Call me doltish and brutal, but I conducted my interactions with a fly rod— stalking the fish, studying their habits, fooling them with devious little baits that I concocted from steel and feather and thread, playing them on a light leader, catching them, and in most cases releasing them but sometimes killing them and eating their flesh. The trout, of course, never reciprocated my appreciation. They had no frigging desire to interact with *me*. But trout are predators too. If they didn't kill and eat insects, small crustaceans, and one another, they wouldn't be susceptible to predation by fly fishermen. That fact is not offered here as an ethical justification for sport fishing. It's just part of the ecological context, worth keeping in mind.

—

Don Thomas, after his first audience with that first cat, became a lion hunter of much the same sort and much the same motivation as me the fisherman. He taught himself some of the requisite skills, and he learned a great deal more at the elbow of a friend called Rosey—full name, John Roseland—who has hunted lions in central Montana for twenty years. Rosey is an amiable fortyish fellow, a seasonal firefighter with long hair and a wrestler's build, who does his own taxidermy and sometimes takes his white toy poodle, as well as his hounds, into the field on a hunt. By Thomas's testimony, Rosey Roseland has forgotten more about mountain lions than most big-mammal biologists will ever know. Thomas himself and Rosey and just a few other friends now constitute the fellowship of serious lion hunters in their area. They all use traditional archery. Sometimes they practice catch-and-release lion hunting. Sometimes they kill an animal and eat it. If they do kill, the hide is salvaged also and becomes a mounted specimen, though that's not the ultimate object of the process. Rosey has two in his trophy room, including one magnificent tom that went almost 170 pounds, plus another hide now being tanned. The hide in tanning once wrapped the body of a lion that Rosey killed this past December, with Thomas as partner to the chase. They shared the meat. That's the animal whose backstrap is presently featured on Thomas's stove, and Rosey, in recognition of his kill shot as well as for other reasons, has joined us tonight for dinner.

During my own fishing years, I never took a trout to a taxidermist. But I can't claim that as any consolation to the animals that I ate. Nor would I argue for any absolute ethical distinction between the killing of a mountain lion and the killing of a trout. If warm blood and fur and mammary glands are enough to set the lion into an exalted category, then we're just back to the old anthropocentric standard of value that has justified such man-against-nature havoc on this planet. The real distinction to be drawn between *Felis concolor* and *Salmo clarki*, if any, is ecological. Is the native trout common within its ecosystem? If so, then perhaps we can afford to eat it. Is the native lion rare? If so, then perhaps we shouldn't. But even the answers to those conditional questions, as it turns out, are far from simple.

Don Thomas and I have corresponded for a year, since he found himself infuriated by something I wrote. It was an essay about the ecological limits faced by large-bodied predators, such as mountain lions, and it contained, in addition to my efforts at scientific explication, some shoot-from-the-hip sarcasm on the subject of lion hunting. To wit: if mountain lions in the northern Rockies are as rare as they *seem* to be, maybe the state fish-and-game regulations shouldn't allow hundreds each year to be "shot for the sheer hell of it and converted to rec-room adornments." I also mentioned that, after many years in Montana, I'd never seen one of these animals in the wild. Written originally for my *Outside* magazine "Natural Acts" column, the essay was later reprinted by a wilderness-advocacy organization to which Thomas belongs. The organization heard from him, promptly and caustically. One part of the message, as relayed onward to me, was essentially this: if that ignorant yuppie wants to *learn* something about mountain lions, he ought to look over a lion hunter's shoulder.

Although I'm too old, insufficiently professional, and not quite urban enough to be a yuppie, the shoe otherwise fit, so I thought I'd wear it. I wrote to Dr. Thomas: Yes, thanks, when do we leave? He wrote back, quite affably, and we made plans to go tracking with his dog.

———

The mountain lion, aka cougar, aka puma and panther, was once the most widely distributed land mammal in the Western Hemisphere, ranging from the Yukon to the southern tip of mainland Chile. It has long since been exterminated almost everywhere in the eastern United States (though a tiny population holds on in southern Florida and there are occasional reports of a lionlike apparition in New England). In the West it has fared better, not for lack of enemies but most likely because the conditions of habitat and the sparseness of human settlement permitted its survival.

From the pioneer days until just thirty years ago, mountain lions in the western states were slaughtered remorselessly, to the point of eradication in some parts of their range and severe reduction in most others. Stockmen hated them, and bounty hunters were paid to shoot as many as possible. During the first three-quarters of this century, the documented tally alone came to 66,665 dead lions. But several factors seem to have saved the western populations from being killed off entirely. Mountain lions are elusive enough, under most circumstances, to avoid contact with humans. They have a relatively high rate of reproduction. Their food supply—mainly mule deer and whitetails—has cycled upward to the point of abundance. The payment of bounties was finally ended. The indiscriminate poisoning of predators with Compound 1080 was curtailed. In 1965, Colorado became the first state to reclassify the lion as a game animal. Other states followed, including Montana in 1971. One effect of this last factor, the change from varmint status to game-animal status, was that it gave hunters a stake in the conservation of *Felis concolor*.

In the four years since I wrote the column that angered Don Thomas, prevailing wisdom on the population status of mountain lions in the northern Rockies has changed. Possibly their actual status has changed too, within those few years, though the current trend goes back several decades. And my own awareness of the particulars has deepened at least slightly. This is not a retraction, then, but it is an admission of incompleteness. Most biologists now seem to agree that populations of *Felis concolor* in the northern Rockies have increased dramatically within the last thirty years. A pleasant surprise, running counter to most other trends in the struggle to conserve jeopardized species: we've got more lions than we used to, it seems. The kill rate attributable to sport hunters is probably no direct threat to the demographic health of the species.

Other factors are. Some stockmen continue to argue for government-funded eradication of mountain lions. And home-in-the-country fever continues to afflict more and more people, especially the recent arrivals from faraway cities, who imagine that a cabin on forty acres in the foothills, a four-by-four rig, a pair of hand-tooled boots, and a dip of Skoal will give them some sort of spiritual rebirth. This phenomenon is probably destroying as much wild landscape, as much lion habitat, as any other factor. It's more permanent than clear-cutting, it's more heedless than Compound 1080, and it's very damn hard to control. It's turning Montana into a cross between Walden and Levittown.

Accidental encounters between humans and lions are also increasing, and a few of those encounters have yielded human fatalities. That sort of thing will bring the lion new trouble. As it becomes more numerous, more constricted by human encroachment on its habitat, and possibly (for reasons still unclear) less shy, *Felis concolor* will risk triggering a campaign of retributive control. Don Thomas has noticed intimations of that in his own community. "People are just talking about it now," he says. "But the first time a lion does something here—whacks a kid, or whatever it happens to be—there's gonna be a tremendous amount of pressure brought to bear to reduce the mountain lion population." He hopes it doesn't happen. He takes joy in knowing that the woods are full of lions.

One morning last winter he tracked a female and her three yearlings in a coulee within walking distance of his house. After treeing them with his dog, he took a few photos and then let them be. It wasn't the day for a kill. When word leaked into town that Dr. Thomas had had four lions at bay—virtually in the suburbs, for Christ's sake—and had intentionally let them escape, some of the good citizens were unhappy.

Some were merely puzzled. Is this guy Thomas a lion killer, or isn't he? The answer to that one is yes.

—

In the depth of winter, with deer season closed and snow piling up in the coulees, Don Thomas and I spend two days together, looking for mountain lions and common ground. We leave town each morning before dawn and drive far into the mountains, with his bluetick hound, Drive, in the back of the pickup. Each day we cover a long stretch of deserted roads, fighting through drifts, scanning the borrow pit and the shoulder for fresh tracks. We hike and ski through some lovely country. We investigate a handful of his favorite spots—places where, as he knows from experience, a lion is likely to cross—while Drive, with his nose high, reads the aromatic Braille of the breezes. The wind is up, with another blizzard reportedly on its way. The air is just cold enough to focus a person's brain. Lunch freezes in my pack, and so does the canteen. As we ski, hike, and drive, we also talk.

Don mentions certain cases of "bad logging" that are ravaging habitat in these mountains, and of "bad mining" that are leaving heavy metals in some of the streams. At another moment, he adds that "one of the biggest impending tragedies" in the struggle waged by conservation organizations, to his mind, "is the polarization between the hunting and nonhunting factions of those groups." This polarization divides resources, it divides people, it wastes time and money, he says. Until hunting and nonhunting conservationists can find the pragmatic wisdom to accommodate each other within the larger fold, he says, "the developers and the miners and the loggers have gotta be laughing all the way to the bank." We also discuss home-in-the-country fever, about which he shares my concern. To both of us it seems maddeningly obvious that if everyone who purports to cherish wild landscape decides they must own and live on a chunk of it, there won't be any more wild landscape. But how do you tackle that problem when the new home-in-the-country developments are full of well-meaning people—conscientious hunters, ethical vegetarians, Sierra Club members—some of whom you personally know and love? Don has no answer, nor do I. In two days of searching, we don't see a single lion, either. But he has convinced me that they're here to be found. Maybe the hard answers are too.

With no lions showing themselves for my benefit, my interaction with *Felis concolor* is limited to the culinary mode, God help me. Back at Don's house, I stand beside his kitchen island, in my hungry ambivalence, while he stirs those medallions in the wok. I watch him dump the pineapple chunks and the julienned peppers into the skillet along with the cubes of flesh and then bring that dish abubble in a pungent gravy. I listen to Rosey describing his own day's effort—he cut the tracks of four different lions, followed them in befuddling circles on a ridge, never spotted an animal in the flesh—and his own paradoxical feelings toward the species. Some of his neighbors have suggested to Rosey, as they have to Don, that if he's such a lion hunter, he ought to exterminate the local population. "Kill them all?" says Rosey. "Hell, that's the last thing I want to do." It's been a good day for Rosey, today, because he went into the woods and worked up a sweat and found evidence that he was in the company of *Felis concolor*. Let's eat, says Don.

He sets two steaming platters before us on the table: sweet-and-sour mountain lion, and mountain lion in black bean sauce.

He pours a nice chardonnay. Before anyone has touched a serving spoon, he raises his glass. "To the animals," says Don Thomas. This is tradition between him and Rosey, who raises his own glass. "To the animals." I raise mine. To the animals. And then we eat. It's the sacrament of accommodation and alliance.

Nothing but a Hound Dog: Cats, Dogs, and Cultural Conflicts

by E. Donnall Thomas, Jr.

Fresh snow always has a tale to tell. After a winter storm, the only way an animal can avoid leaving a record of its activities is to fly or sit still. The wildlife has been active overnight, and after two hours studying the dots and dashes flowing past the headlights, the sudden appearance of the track we are seeking feels like the discovery of a gold nugget at the bottom of a pan. As we slide to a stop, coffee cups and Pop-Tarts—the official Breakfast of Lion Hunters—scatter everywhere. After I tumble from the truck, the cold morning air feels like aftershave lotion slapped across my checks. It is wonderful to be outside at last.

To many, the track would be nothing but another disturbance

in the snow, but experience has taught us better. The prints look as round as saucers, and their measured stride suggests confidence and purpose. Out here in the open, the deep powder makes it difficult to evaluate their size. Flashlights in hand, Rosey and I follow them down into the trees along the creek, where the snow is more compact and revealing. Even there the verdict is equivocal. The lion might be a tom, but it might be a female. What the hell: the dogs need the exercise, and so do we.

Back at the truck, we load our packs and discuss strategy. This morning, we are an eclectic crew. If lion hunting had an equivalent of the esteemed (and, according to most indications, soon to be extinct) British Master of Fox Hounds, John "Rosey" Roseland would be one. He was hunting cougars in these hills before the idea even occurred to anyone else. On the other end of the spectrum, Ann Williams has never seen a mountain lion. She is here this morning because of curiosity and friendship and, I suspect, because she has figured out that running up and down mountains does as much for you as running up and down StairMasters, with the additional benefit of superior scenery. With a decade of hounds and lions under my belt, I fall somewhere on Rosey's side of the midline.

Tucked away in the back of the truck, the more experienced dogs have already figured out what's up, and an excited clamor greets us as we throw down the tailgate. I snap a leash on Drive, my bluetick hound, and walk him to the track while Rosey follows suit with his dog, Charlie. Both of them like what they smell. Turning Drive loose feels like launching a warm-blooded cruise missile. Back at the truck, Ann has instructions to hang on to the rest of the dogs; but that's too much to ask of anyone, and as Drive and Charlie charge down the slope and across the creek, the young dogs escape her grasp and tumble along behind.

Ignoring the urge to shoulder my pack and get on with things, I stand in the snow and listen. Lion hunts are long-distance affairs guided for the most part by nothing more dramatic than tracks in the snow, and I don't get to listen to my hounds as much as I might like except at the beginning and the end. Somewhere out there in the gloom, Drive's mellow baritone marks the leading edge of the chase. Because I have raised him from a puppy, I close my eyes and follow his progress with pride even though there is no way anyone but God can take any credit for that incredible nose. Charlie's bawl sounds steady and competent as always. Somewhere behind them, Axle, Rosey's second black-and-tan, chimes in with his distinctive high-pitched bleat. I like to imagine that Pete, my young dog, is adding his voice somewhere to the chorus, although if pressed I would admit that might be wishful thinking.

Finally they are out of earshot, their lovely voices lost to the mountain wind. High overhead, the dark peak looms, eclipsing the first warm glow of the sunrise. The sweet part is over. As we collect our gear, we debate the need for snowshoes. No one wants to bother with them, but I elect to hedge my bets by strapping mine behind my pack. Then there is nothing left to do but begin the long, uncertain climb uphill into the darkness.

—

Forget guard dogs and shepherds, pointers and setters. Historically, the essential relationship between man and working dogs is best defined by hounds.

Ever since some distant human ancestor first stood on two legs and picked up a stick, *Homo sapiens* has enjoyed only two advantages over the rest of the competition in the food chain: a prehensile thumb and a brain (and only one of those works consistently). On the other hand, the animals our forebears longed to eat (and the animals that longed to eat them) were their overwhelming superiors in sight, hearing, smell, speed, and strength. The logical remedy was to enlist some assistance. *Voilà*: hounds.

Edward Steichen's spectacular photographic collection *The Family of Man* contains an arresting shot of a Kalahari tribesman about to plunge a spear into the chest of a gemsbok his dogs have brought to bay. The composition is fraught with tension: the hunter looks pitifully small next to the gemsbok, and it is hard to avoid the feeling that all hell is about to break loose. *This says it all*, I thought as soon as I saw that picture. *A hungry hunter. A dangerous quarry. Some damn good dogs.* No doubt a victim of my own instincts, the rest of the collection scarcely seemed to matter.

By the time of the American Revolution, hound hunting in the British Isles had already undergone a paradoxical transition from the realm of the hunter-gatherer to defining pastime of the upper classes. In fact, it is precisely that element of snobbery that underlies the modern drive to ban hound hunting in England, a movement that has less to do with foxes and hounds than with class resentment and the marginalization of rural values in an increasingly urban society. Outdoorsmen on this side of the Atlantic should certainly take note. The more any activity becomes the exclusive province of the privileged, the harder it is to defend in an egalitarian society.

Of course, early Americans saw things differently. In my own revisionist view of history, I sometimes suspect that the American Revolution had more to do with hunting rights than unfair taxes. At any rate, hounds were an integral part of America's outdoor heritage from the beginning, especially in the South, where the gentry raised hounds to hunt bears for sport and sharecroppers used them to put 'possum pie on the table.

Regional biases were an important factor in hound hunting's eventual fall from cultural grace. The end of the Civil War marked a period of general disenchantment with southern cultural values, during which it was all too easy for outside arbiters of taste to associate hound hunting with evils as diverse as chewing tobacco and Jim Crow racism. Remember how the press once pilloried Lyndon Johnson for having the bad judgment to tug on a beagle's ears in front of a camera? The ruckus wasn't really as much about the hound as it was about Johnson's refusal to check his down-home cultural values at the door when he moved into the White House.

These attitudes laid the foundation for the current assault on hound hunting by animal rights activists. Give the devil his due; today's organized opponents of hunting know how to play the media like a fiddle, and they have convinced a remarkable number of naive and misinformed voters that hound hunting is a barbaric cultural relic that should be banned as we move forward toward a Brave New World of vegetarianism. An outdoor columnist with whom I have butted heads over this matter in print once labeled hunters' concerns over such loss of rights hysterical. Hysteria is an unreasonable fear. Try explaining this alleged unreasonableness to houndsmen in California, Oregon, and Washington, where political correctness has turned good lion dogs into pot-lickers forever.

The traditional anti-hunting elements of modern society aren't the only ones to question the propriety of hunting cougars with dogs, an activity that occasionally raises eyebrows among hunters themselves. Because of my own deep commitment to traditional bow hunting—arguably the most demanding and nuance-laden hunting method of all—I've listened to my share of criticism from skilled bow hunters who think lion hunting with hounds consists of nothing more than following a pack of dogs to a tree in order to shoot a helpless cat. In fact, while lion hunting can certainly be reduced to a charade by overuse of machines and gadgets, in its purest form it demands as much skill and physical effort as any outdoor activity I know.

At least skeptics in this group can usually be educated. I have far less patience with the objections to lion hunting that come from those young, affluent, nonhunting outdoor enthusiasts who think that owning a pair of hiking boots and subscribing to a few trendy magazines makes them authorities on wildlife. (I once accused the author of another chapter in this collection of harboring such biases. As his contribution makes clear, we eventually worked out our differences over a mountain lion dinner.) To many members of this set, the idea of shooting a mountain lion under any circumstances evokes the kind of revulsion most societies reserve for matters of religious heresy. Most cite biology as the basis of their convictions. Never mind that these individuals and the institutions they support think nothing of patronizing destination ski resorts carved from winter habitat critical to the survival of deer, elk, and cougars. Actually, I think the real offense stems from the failure of most lion hunters to acknowledge the most important principle in the yuppie canon of outdoor ethics: the absolute necessity of looking great in the latest fashionable outdoor wear.

All of which helps explain why I'm not just going hunting when I load my pack and start up the mountain after the dogs this morning. Like any other disenfranchised member of society, I am defending my own cultural values and way of life.

—

It has already been a long winter, and several cycles of freezing and thawing have left a treacherous layer of ice beneath the new snow, which makes the long climb up the mountain a classical exercise in the "two steps forward, one step back" school of locomotion. The rocks are treacherous, and at times we are reduced to traveling on hands and knees. Pete has lost the chase and doubled back, adding additional confusion to the jumble of tracks weaving back and forth across the mountainside. But every time the trail seems uncertain, we spread out and study the sign, and somewhere in the riot of dog tracks we always manage to find the cat's. Despite the silence up ahead, the chase is still on.

There are ways to make this process easier. You can outfit the lead dogs with radio collars and use snow machines to shorten the track, all of which makes chasing lions a lot more like a video game and a lot less like hunting. As someone once said: *include me out.* The dignity of lion hunting is inseparable from its difficulty. Take away the woodsmanship, the tracking skills, and the burning legs, and the hunt is soon reduced to an execution. Some cats have eluded us over the years because of our stubborn adherence to this principle, but I don't need to kill anything badly enough to justify its compromise. It's a wonder that anyone does.

As we finally begin to close upon the ridgeline, the sun breaks through the trees and the breeze starts to freshen. Although the morning has actually become quite pleasant, wind and rising temperature mean difficult scenting conditions for the dogs. To make matters worse, the exposed ridge is almost bare of tracking snow. We follow the track to a barren cliff, where it finally disappears in the rocks. Our ears tell us nothing. The dogs are out there somewhere, but the mountains seem impossibly vast and indifferent. *Shit.* There is just no other word to describe the situation, not after the long climb and the realization that our dogs are missing in action.

After a brief strategy discussion, I set off around the cliffs to see if the track has gone on over the ridge, while Rosey and Ann skirt the side hill below. Within minutes, we are out of contact. If all goes well, one of us will find the track and the chase intact, and we can get on with the business of trying to tree the lion. If all does not go well, we may spend the next week combing the mountains for the dogs.

The critics may call lion hunting many things, but I defy them to accuse it of being easy.

———

In some parts of the country, folks tend to go on and on about their hounds like soccer moms going on about their children. While I genuinely like my hounds, I'm perfectly willing to be realistic about their limitations. Perhaps I've just spent too much time with Labrador retrievers, but from stink to stupidity, the list of generic hound faults sometimes seems overwhelming. In fact, a good hound can expect to have only five things in its favor: four legs and a nose. Additional positive qualities usually exist only in the imagination of the handler. As Elvis once reminded us in song, it's hard to beat a hound dog as an icon for slouching opportunism.

I came by my affection for hounds the old-fashioned way: I inherited it. As a kid, my father chased all manner of game around north Texas river bottoms with his dogs before he went on to other things, including, eventually, the Nobel Prize in medicine. (So much for the houndsman's conventional Bubba stereotype.) I got to listen to those stories around the fireplace when I was a kid myself, and the reading matter my family shared by the same fireplace was as likely to include *The Voice of Bugle Ann* as Shakespeare. In fact, enthusiasm for hounds has always depended upon just the kind of tradition that is best handed down through generations. The odd thing is how strongly our multicultural society has endorsed the validity of some cultural traditions at the expense of others.

In contrast to most contemporary sporting breeds, hounds hunt with us rather than for us, an attitude that tends to alienate bird dog handlers, who are accustomed to a certain measure of subservience in the field. In their defense, I can only describe the performance of good hounds on a track as a miracle. As members of a species that has somehow outgrown its own sense of smell, we should view with awe a hound's ability to stick its nose into a day-old lion track and follow the smell into the next county. The sensory cues that define such a performance are immeasurable, and all the king's horses of the modern computer age remain incapable of reproducing it, no small reassurance to those troubled by the notion that technology has rendered instinct obsolete. Anyone who shares my own discomfort with cyberspace should be able to regard a determined hound running a track as a cause for celebration.

—

Following the trail of a lion chase is essentially an exercise in logic. Circling through the snow on the far side of the blown-out ridge reveals no sign of a lion track, and if the dogs had the cat treed nearby, I would hear them. Ergo, they must have gone below.

After picking my way back down through the rocks, I angle

through the trees until I can confirm the hypothesis. The first canine print is circling aimlessly through the pines, and I suspect that it belongs to Pete, who hasn't quite got the hang of this yet. A hundred yards farther across the hill, his track joins a jumble of others and I pause to sort them out in the snow. They belong to three more dogs, the cat, Ann, and Rosey. When I stop and listen hard above the sound of the wind in the trees, I can finally hear the crisp, staccato chop of the dogs at the tree. Somewhere down in the dark reaches of the canyon below, the chase is over.

Slipping and sliding down the fall line, I arrive at the base of a towering ponderosa to find Ann and Rosey staring into the branches overhead. At the base of the tree, Axle and Charlie are doing their best to become airborne. Drive, whose strength has always been on the track rather than at the tree, is yapping away indifferently while Pete trots in circles looking for faces to lick. The best I can hope for the pup today is that he has learned something.

And then there is the cat. No matter how many times I stare up into an evergreen canopy and see a mountain lion, I doubt that I will ever become accustomed to the experience, and to tell the truth, I hope I never do. Tawny and graceful, the cat looks as if it belongs on another continent, if not another planet. Remarkably indifferent to the ruckus at ground level, it is studying us coldly, as if it knows it could bound down out of the tree and kill us all at will, which, since we are unarmed except for longbows, is probably quite true.

So why is the cougar sitting passively overhead? It turns out that the familiar animosity between dogs and cats far preceded their domestication. Recent field studies suggest that in areas where their ranges overlap, wolves drive cougars away from over half their kills and claim them for themselves (a fact that advocates of wolf recovery conveniently chose to ignore while assessing the biological impact of the gray wolf's reintroduction to the northern Rockies). While a grown cougar can hold its own against anything in the woods, lions are solitary animals that never emulated the canine instinct for hunting in packs. Cougars evolved in the New World prior to the arrival of humans, which meant that climbing trees effectively removed them from the reaches of all their naturally occurring predators. Our cat is simply doing what its instincts have taught it.

The chase may be over, but the hunt is not. The kill may come as something of an anticlimax at the end of a long, uncertain trail, but it is still an integral part of the event and it must be dealt with, like the final act of a play or the sword at the end of a bullfight. However, there is still one important issue to resolve, for we do not yet know the sex of the cat. That can be a difficult determination to make, especially when the anatomically correct object of scrutiny is tucked away high in the branches of a pine tree. Rosey finally has to shinny all the way up the tree to confirm the fact of the matter. As it turns out, the cat is a female.

The quota in this district is still open, and there are many reasons for one of us to string a bow and shoot the lion. The cat is as big a female as Rosey and I have ever seen. Killing her would provide the dogs with a welcome conclusion to the hunt, and after the long chase, there is no doubt that they have earned one. Female lions often have nicer hides than males, and they taste better on the table. I don't know a single local rancher who wouldn't be delighted to have one less cougar in the hills. The problem is that I just don't want to kill a female and neither does Rosey. After an appropriate period of discussion, we dig the leashes out of our packs and begin the process of dragging the disappointed hounds away from the tree. In contrast to the dogs, Ann is plainly relieved by our decision.

Personally, I'm satisfied to write off the long morning as just another day of catch-and-release lion hunting.

—

The best thing to be said for the long walk off the mountain is that it's all downhill. The footing is even worse than it was during the climb, and the dogs seem to think their leashes were meant to let them amuse themselves by hog-tying their handlers. By the time we reach the truck, we are all bruised and battered, and I have enough snow and pine needles down the back of my jacket to make my skin crawl. Without a lion hide or hindquarters in my pack, it's hard not to wonder if it's all been worth it.

Pleasantly exhausted, the dogs seem happy to return to the security of their kennel. Back inside the truck, we round up enough leftover junk food to replenish a few of the calories we burned on our way up the mountain. Even the cold coffee tastes good. Although no one has enough energy left to express it, the shared feeling is one of accomplishment. As we turn the truck around to face the long road home, each of us seems to understand that we have witnessed something special and timeless. And as it turns out, I'm glad the lion is still up there somewhere.

Just as I hope that we will be able to do this again, and to pass the value of the experience along to the next generation.

The Deer
with the Long Tail

by Diane Josephy Peavey

It was 1985 when Raoul, our Peruvian sheepherder, while walking through aspen meadows to check his band of sheep early one summer morning, came upon thirty-five dead ewes and lambs. The day before, he had spotted a mountain lion when he was moving the band through High Five Canyon on our ranch. Still, he was caught off guard by the sight of so much carnage. Denny, our sheep manager of thirty years, confirmed it was a mountain lion when he arrived later that day: the sheep were killed at the neck, several of them dragged off and covered, almost buried, in brush. These are the signs of a mountain lion.

From a distance, High Five Canyon is little more than a

furrow along the ridgeline between our large, remote Idaho sheep and cattle ranch and the busy resort community of the Wood River Valley, home to Sun Valley. But up close, High Five is a deep, wide canyon with fir and aspen clinging to the face of its steep slopes. Meadows fill the bottom country. It is still peaceful and undisturbed on our side of the mountains.

Our ranch, at 6,000 feet, is made up of draws like High Five and stretches of pasturelands that stay green late into the summer. This open country is home to deer, antelope, and elk. Sage hens and sandhill cranes nest on our meadows. Coyotes roam the hills. Several years ago, my husband spotted a wolf in the wild. He has seen mountain lions, but not often.

When Denny talks about the cougar attack even now, thirteen years later, there is surprise and fear in his voice. Like his father Dennis, who was also our sheep manager for years, Denny knows this landscape and its wildlife well. He tells me, "During all my growing up, I don't remember ever seeing a mountain lion. They were there, but you didn't see them."

He stops. "No, there was one. When I was a kid, I saw him when I was riding to town with Dad. I didn't know what it was. 'Look at that deer with the long tail,' I pointed. Dad laughed. 'It's a mountain lion,' he told me."

The cougar kill in 1985 was a wake-up call for us. Although it was not the first on our ranch, it coincided with a dramatic increase in cougar sightings and livestock kills throughout the region. Clearly, the wildlife balance was shifting, predation increasing.

Today the problem is apparent. Numbers of mountain lions are on the rise, and as they compete with each other to survive, they are depleting the traditional food sources. Forced to search out new prey, they become increasingly visible near human habitation.

And there is hard evidence to confirm what was originally anecdotal information. In 1990 the state of Idaho began a depredation program to reimburse ranchers for animal death loss. A family could be compensated for anything over a $1,000 loss.

This amount, department managers reasoned, would attest to the severity of the attack. Wildlife specialists from the U.S. Fish and Wildlife Service verify the kill before the state will reimburse the rancher. They confirm the manner of death and identify the predator.

In 1990, at the beginning of the state program, the Idaho Department of Fish and Game recorded the stories of, and compensated seven ranchers for, mountain lion losses. In 1994, the number of reimbursements doubled to fourteen. Two years later there were fifty-seven cases. Each case involved substantial numbers of sheep.

A look at several of the case files gives names, numbers, and locations to these losses. One morning in April 1996, for example, Roger Oxarango went out to his field near the south central Idaho town of Minidoka and found eighty-nine lambs and four ewes killed by a mountain lion. I try to imagine coming upon such a scene of devastation, but I can't.

That same year the Etcheverrys and Binghams lost thirty lambs and seven ewes in southeastern Idaho. In May 1997, the Soulen family lost sixty-seven lambs and six ewes in the Crane Creek desert country, and in September they found another twenty-eight lambs and five ewes killed on their summer range outside of McCall. Both locations were in western Idaho. These experiences confirmed the increasing number of mountain lions and the geography over which these animals now roamed.

"I've seen cats where I've never seen them before," says Laird Noh, a third-generation sheep rancher and Idaho state senator. He chairs the Environment and Natural Resources Committee in the Senate and has long been recognized by environmentalists and ranchers for his knowledge and reasoned approach to resource issues.

Noh doesn't hide his concern over the rise in mountain lion numbers. "They have taken out many of the bighorn sheep in the south hills," he says of his home range country. And Noh's livestock operation is not without loss. Eight sheep in one week, seven the next, all cougar kills. Then, several days later, more than eighty animals suffocated when a stalking cat chased a group of frightened lambs and ewes downhill into a dense wall of aspen where, in panic, they piled on the lead animals.

Steve Huffaker, chief of wildlife at the Department of Fish and Game, explains the increasing number of lion attacks this way. As Idaho and surrounding states ban or limit the hunting of mountain lions, these socially solitary creatures, now in greater numbers, must compete for traditional food sources. They often cover hundreds of miles in their search. They travel alone, avoiding their fiercest competitor, another mountain lion. These altered life patterns are taking a toll on wildlife. According to Huffaker, mountain lions have all but killed off mule deer and bighorn sheep in areas of Idaho and now are seriously affecting elk populations. As these food sources become scarce, cats expand their prey base, moving into new environments.

In south central Idaho, cougars have been seen attacking small farm flocks near the town of Castleford and walking brazenly across the Blue Lakes golf course just outside the city of Twin Falls. From around the state have come reports of attacks on dogs and llamas and sightings around suburban Boise homes, where children recently treed one of these cats.

In Sun Valley a mountain lion and her yearling cub killed a pet llama, and for days the cougars were seen perched on the kill, feasting on the buried remains, while neighbors gathered to photograph the event.

On another occasion, my husband and I were called to an expensive Sun Valley home to rescue, or rather remove, a ewe—not ours, as it turned out—from the basement of the house. The very large sheep, we determined, had sought refuge in the pink and lavender bedroom, jumping through the ground-level window while fleeing a fearsome foe. "We *have* seen mountain lions in the area," the couple told us almost apologetically as we coaxed the terrified ewe up the white carpeted stairs and through the tiled foyer to our pickup parked under the front portico.

For my part, I have never seen a cougar in the wild. Nor have I seen the bodies of lambs or llamas ripped open and hidden away under brush after a mountain lion kill. Both must be unforgettable sights. But it will only get worse for the cats, as well as for the lambs, dogs, and perhaps even children who become prey, as the cougar numbers increase and their habitat disappears. For those of us who live on the land, it is part of another tragedy, the erosion of our landscape and our lives as they are compromised to development. Almost daily, villages become towns and towns become cities, reaching deeply into our open space.

Follow the predator losses on the map and you will trace the regions of new growth. Sheep have moved through these areas for close to 100 years, rarely disturbed by mountain lions, but that was before housing developments were built to the edge of and into the foothills. Today there are fewer and fewer places to breathe and roam free. We lose our balance, humans and wildlife alike.

I am convinced that those of us living on the land may be the greatest deterrent to careless new growth. While we remain, we are the keepers of open space and habitat, obstacles to reckless expansion. And we become vilified on the chance we might leave.

But those of us who live here gain our strength from wildlands. It is why we stay, even in the face of punishing economic odds. And although we are horrified at the sight of dead lambs in a mountain meadow, we are also appalled by the confusion of housing and industrial sites crowding the edges of our lives. So we hold out for open space, hoping that in the end it will save us, wildlife and humans alike.

Sign

by Harley G. Shaw

The track was in moist sand, one of the few soft spots along the rock-strewn Arizona canyon called Conger Water. I was glad Ginny saw the track first; she waved in controlled excitement for me to come and confirm it. Her hopes had been high too many times before but this was it, the track of a mature, female mountain lion. For the next hour Ginny photographed it, measured it, and absorbed its image.

Ginny lived near Boston. Although no cougar population has existed in Massachusetts for 150 years, people still see them, or think they do, and Ginny had been investigating the sightings. Anecdotes were not sufficient, no matter how credible the observer. She demanded proof: pictures, tracks, or a cougar—living or dead. After responding to hundreds of reports, she had not yet seen hard evidence. Either cougars weren't there, or Ginny couldn't recognize cougar sign when she saw it.

She contacted me to eliminate the latter possibility. She wanted to see cougar tracks, to confirm her ability to identify them, and to sense the chance of finding tracks where cougars were known to still exist. In Arizona, we know we have lions. I had just finished eight years of research, capturing mountain lions with the help of hounds, fitting them with radio collars, and following them to the prey they killed. With three other trackers, I had been working to estimate the density of lions in various Arizona habitats and to evaluate the track count as a method for monitoring lion populations. Ginny wanted badly to see one track; we had looked at thousands over the years.

So Ginny joined us on a survey in the Sierra Ancha Mountains, but in an entire week, searching good tracking surfaces in the best of lion country, we found no lion sign. Sometimes it happens that way. We found coyote, bobcat, and black bear tracks along with the expected deer, peccary, and smaller mammals; Ginny's ability to spot these convinced me she was not missing sign on her home ground. She had a tracker's eye. Nevertheless, she returned to Massachusetts with no cougar track to her credit.

But Ginny was determined. She returned the following fall to stay at our home in Chino Valley. From there we could go to Spider Ranch, where I had done my initial research. I knew how lions moved through this country. On the first morning out, we found an imprint at Conger Water. The following day, we found sign of another female with small kittens, and my dogs sniffed out the remains of a deer that the family had killed and eaten.

Fifteen years have passed since Ginny's visits, and Massachusetts has yet to produce a cougar population. Ginny moved west and now volunteers her time on field studies of lions in California. She has not only seen tracks but observed living, wild lions.

Ginny's short visits to Arizona initiated a change in my own view of lions and their sign. Before, I had seen sign simply as a scientist's means of gathering data. But Ginny traveled to Arizona because there were no lions left where she lived. As I continued my own surveys, lion sign took on a different significance. I realized that studying lion sign was a special opportunity, for without knowing lion sign, you can't know lions—the cats are rarely seen even where there are plenty around. I know ranchers, hunters, and woodsmen who have spent their lives in good lion country and have never seen a living lion, but they see sign and will tell you lions are abundant. People unskilled in seeing lion sign may assume, often incorrectly, that lions are scarce.

Our own field research seldom involved direct observation of the cats. We caught and radio-marked them with the aid of dogs; then, once released, the lions resumed their invisibility, identified only by a particular radio pulse. When we were later guided toward them by directional antennas, we often failed to see lions that we knew were only yards away. More often than not, we left the animals unseen, even though the radio signal told us they had not moved.

We learned early that lions would lie and watch, allowing humans, and undoubtedly other creatures, to move around them. Unless pushed by scent hounds or, rarely, confronted with the direct gaze of a radio-toting biologist, they seldom fled. Seeing a lion, even where they were common, was unusual. We learned to rely on tracks and other forms of sign to determine their behavior.

One of the cowboys who helped us capture lions frequently reported seeing "lots of deer down on Sycamore Mesa" or "two bear, a sow and a cub, in Conger Water" on days he worked alone. I began to question his honesty, since we never saw so many animals when riding together. Then one day I was present when he reported to his wife that he and I had seen "two female lions in Cottonwood Canyon," and the light came on. He was reporting tracks. To him, the sign and the animal were the same.

Tracking is part of American folklore. Our heroes, from Natty Bumppo, the fictional protagonist of James Fenimore Cooper's *Leatherstocking Tales*, to Daniel Boone, to mountain men such as Jim Bridger or Kit Carson, could read sign like we read headlines. After working alongside a few old lion hunters, I can testify that some people do become extremely skilled at reading the faint traces animals leave behind.

Such finely turned abilities do not happen without need, and few modern individuals need such skills. Tracking was an adaptation prompted by living close to the land and is no longer a part of what we do.

While we have tuned into the complex signals of urban life and can read certain sign in the subway or on the interstate, technology has eliminated the need for sensitivity to wilder environments. If you live in a house with modern heating and cooling, you need not be attuned to the subtleties that announce weather changes—the shifts in sky tone or bird song that tell of coming storms. If you do not hunt or gather food, you no longer must feel or hear signals that tell you prey or, more important, something that views you as prey, is near. Sensitivity to the undercurrents of the wilds no longer has adaptive value.

In monitoring today's information glut, we have learned to scan for particular titles or for key words. In a similar fashion, the key to seeing natural sign involves focusing on appropriate search images. During my research, I developed a search image for lion tracks, and I am still jerked out of my reveries by anything on the ground that resembles that form. I don't have to think about it. At the peak of our research on lions, I would close my eyes after a day in the field, and the outline of a lion track would shine on my eyelid like a light bulb viewed too long.

I never developed the finer skills needed to follow faint animal traces for miles across barren landscapes. My ability essentially ended at seeing and recognizing. The hounds, with their superior sense of smell, did the trailing. My job was to be sure they were trailing the right species and that they were headed forward, not backward, on the track. On occasion, I would locate a track the dogs had run past and line them out again. I needed the ability to see and identify lion tracks with certainty, but I was far from being a tracker.

Good interpreters of sign are now a rarity, especially in North America. Sign reading skills, in spite of their potential value, are fading within the ranks of biologists responsible for the welfare of wildlife. Antler rubs, browse marks, lion scrapes—all are signs that can reveal a great deal about how animals are using the land and what their needs are. Yet in this era of radio collars and helicopters, we have become dependent upon technology that allows us to monitor many wild species without setting our feet on the ground. We gather specific, management-oriented data quickly and return to our desks and computers. We no longer function within a wild, local landscape, sensing its vital signs because they affect our own well-being. We have become isolated from nature and as a result may apply technology where it isn't needed, habitually relying instead on expensive tools where simple and low-cost observation might suffice. We indulge in technological overkill, at least partly because we have lost our basic ability to see.

Radio-tracking of animals, for example, is a powerful research tool that has added much to our understanding of wildlife. But it has also become a political crutch, used to create an illusion of action rather than to produce facts. It makes good public relations. Wildlife shows and articles cover the sensational aspects of capturing animals and are replete with pictures of antenna-toting biologists listening to beeps in the woods. But for those who depend upon beeps alone—who fail to check the sign—telemetry can be misleading.

In our own lion research, we once plotted daily movements

of a male lion over some twenty square miles, relying upon radio locations provided by an observer in an airplane. After a couple of weeks, however, because we could not locate this animal's tracks nor receive a signal near any of the radio locations we were given, we began to suspect that something was wrong. Upon investigation, we found the lion dead where we had originally marked it. Our dart had ruptured a blood vessel, and the animal bled to death. It had not moved since we attached the radio collar, but the vagaries of the radio signal created misleading results. Our aerial tracker sharpened his technique after that, and we sought ways to improve our capture techniques. We also proceeded with increased faith in the older observational skills.

Habitual dependence upon technology can actually create well-executed studies that do not fulfill their stated goals. The tool begins to direct the research. An example is a study of the effects of logging on an isolated Arizona wild turkey population that was conducted because a local group of citizens opposed a timber sale. Turkeys were identified as a species of concern, and the U.S. Forest Service agreed to fund turkey research before any additional cutting of trees would be allowed. Although agency biologists (myself included) suggested that a short-term radio-tracking study would not provide the needed information, a graduate student was nonetheless assigned to capture and attach radios to a small number of the birds. The student was given no say in the design. Half the radio-marked birds died within two weeks after they were trapped, and the remaining small sample of birds spent little time on the area to be logged— although based upon tracks and feeding sign, a larger, unmarked segment of the turkey population did. The end result was that the student wasn't able to monitor distribution of the total turkey population on and around the timber sale area, a task that probably could have been accomplished by systematically monitoring sign. For the agencies involved, the image of doing high-tech research was more important than the goals of the study.

Recommendations supporting the use of simple, nonintrusive, observational techniques were ignored.

I don't believe that this is an unusual situation. Much of the work of biologists today deals with the effects of commercial or sporting uses on wildlife—logging, grazing, land development, recreation, hunting. A common approach in determining the impact of such activities is to hang a few radios on some key species of concern, observe behavior patterns associated with the specified land uses, and then predict the broader effects on an entire wildlife population or even a species. Too often, predictions are based upon information from limited areas covering short spans of time. The information may well be the best available, but it may not encompass the spectrum of habitat or weather conditions that the wild population may ultimately encounter. It may not apply to all situations at all times.

Instead of speculations derived from short-term intensive study and subsequent prediction, what we need in many cases is long-term monitoring of sign. Natural systems are too large and too complex to be studied exclusively through intensive, high-tech research, and their management ultimately must rely upon more subjective judgments based on long observation and experience—long tuning to the background.

I believe that this is where well-trained amateurs could play a role in resource management. With agency biologists forced to manage an increasing variety of species and habitats, and with the documentation and constraints demanded by the National Environmental Policy Act, the Endangered Species Act, and other legislation, fewer and fewer professionals are leaving their desks and going to the woods. They are unable to dig themselves out from under the volume of environmental assessments, environmental impact statements, and other forms of project documentation. Periodic, long-term monitoring of common species seldom occurs. Well-trained lay naturalists with specific skills could do much to lighten this load.

Admittedly, recent trends in biological sciences have not encouraged amateurs. The high-tech approach to research, along with esoteric statistical treatment of data, has created an illusion that worthwhile work is outside the abilities of lay-people. The extreme institutionalization of biology, and all other sciences for that matter, has placed virtually all research under government control. The work of a trained amateur is likely to be ignored due to lack of credentials or title.

Agency people are too busy, and too sophisticated, to monitor animal sign in the woods. Concerned citizens feel unqualified and unauthorized to do fieldwork, yet they lack faith in decisions being made. This expresses itself too often in the excesses of environmental activism.

Many of the demands on the time of professional biologists have been created in part by activists—the people who seemingly are most worried about nature. In many cases, the issues created by such groups, however well intentioned, do little more than increase the paperwork of agency biologists and tie them closer to their desks. Perhaps such activists would do more good if they spent more time in the woods gathering information and less time in meetings, forcing premature political decisions. Perhaps development of observational skills would help to alleviate their anxieties. If nothing else, time so spent would be more enjoyable than the hours spent posturing in the incessant and ineffectual meetings that seem to be a hallmark of our time.

Aldo Leopold, in his essay "Wildlife in American Culture," wrote of the "sport" of doing wildlife research. He expressed hope that a natural evolution would occur in hunters as they matured, from the efficiency of modern weapons to self-imposed limitations of primitive weapons, thence to the camera and, finally, the notebook. I think that our wildlife agencies, perhaps reacting to the threat of uncontrolled expertise, have failed to foster this final stage in the "sportsman's" development. I also believe that nonhunters, the environmentalists if you please, have become too fond of political battle to indulge in simple observation. In our high-tech and adversarial world, we have forgotten that the founders of our environmental knowledge, such as Darwin, Mendel, and Thoreau, were amateurs in the truest sense of the word. They had no biological degrees, no agency titles, no government grants, no official authorization to do research. But they did have excellent eyes, ears, and brains. And they understood the labor of love.

Maybe what I'm trying to say is that we all need to move closer to our subject—to develop the skills required to determine truth for ourselves, or at least to evaluate the information we receive from others. We must continue to refine our skills in order to differentiate between activities that truly threaten wild populations or their habitat, as opposed to those that merely trigger our own territorial reactions to change. We must observe regularly enough and long enough to understand the difference between pulsating natural changes and factors that may truly damage wild populations over long periods. Short-term research is of value only if it has a long-term background for comparison. We need a historical database in order to differentiate carefully between valid issues and the ineffectual turf wars that divert our attention from the land—the background.

Virtually everything we read or view on television represents a continental or global perspective. We know more about environmental conditions in Brazil than about density or distribution of the coyotes, deer, or birds in our backyard. We monitor a worldwide background filtered by the media and develop anxieties derived from the predictions of authorities we've never met. Our judgements become based upon ethical clichés and vague principals, not personal knowledge. And because we are losing the skills required to attain this knowledge, because we have been awed by technology, we may depend too much upon working biologists who are themselves increasingly removed from the land. There is not only room, there is need for skilled amateur naturalists keeping track of conditions at home.

Of course, any lay efforts at monitoring wildlife must be scientifically rigorous. Adequate training by skilled observers is essential. Given such training, amateur naturalists can become an important part of the biological community. The activities of such trained individuals can perhaps be contrasted with past events surrounding the eastern cougar.

Ginny Fifield was not the only person who searched for lions in the East. Many other devoted naturalists, both amateur and professional, have searched for sign in several eastern states. In some cases, lack of training or experience has created confusion. I once joined a team of such worthies to search for cougar tracks in New Brunswick, Canada. In fact, I was invited as a professional lion biologist to give the effort respectability. I was also the official skeptic regarding the presence of lions. New Brunswick lies north of habitats where cougars were historically abundant, and based upon my experience with the animal, I felt that boreal forests and deep snows would probably discourage any cougars that might wander into the province. I also felt that the habitat was now too fragmented to sustain a viable population, and I could see no nearby source for immigrants. Yet people in New Brunswick regularly report sightings of cougars and have done so for decades.

On our trip, we found no tracks. I personally doubt that a lion population has existed in New England or the Maritimes (if any ever existed in the Maritimes) for nearly 200 years. Yet residents of these areas still watch hopefully for cougars.

Because of a flush of unverified sightings, New Brunswick created an eastern panther recovery team designed to manage the limited—and I believe nonexistent—population. Records of sightings are maintained and pins placed on maps showing their locations. But with one possible exception, no solid sign has yet been found. Fifty years ago, Bruce Wright, a wildlife biologist who believed the New Brunswick cats existed, wrote two books on the subject, *Ghost of North America* and *The Eastern Panther*. But he, too, depended upon ephemeral sightings and failed to locate any tangible sign. A cult has developed around his writings—looking, waiting, hoping for a cougar confirmation. I think that his adherents' lack of experience causes them to hope that something that may never have existed has now returned.

With training they could help lay the matter to rest. As it is, they seem to represent a mysticism based on yearnings for species lost, blindly chasing ghost lions because they no longer understand sign. Are they waiting for this symbol from a mythical past to tell them once again that all is well? If so, we are in danger of searching for the dead, while the living slip away unseen.

Bullets, Ballots, and
Predatory Instincts

by Wayne Pacelle

Predators and people haven't mixed well. Take at look at the numbers—or, in the case of the nonhumans, what's left of them. There are about 270 million people in the United States, up from 152 million in 1950 and 76 million in 1900. It's staggering growth, and not about to end.

The large predators, conversely, barely hang on in the conterminous states. While the grizzly bear population was once estimated at 100,000 strong, only about 1,000 to 1,500 grizzlies hold on in the Greater Yellowstone Ecosystem and the Northern Continental Divide Ecosystem, while satellite populations in Idaho and Washington are measured only in the dozens.

Wolves, too, have been more reviled than revered—with only about 2,500 surviving in the contiguous forty-eight states. The once wide-ranging wolf has survived as a continuous population only in the sparsely populated northern reaches of Michigan, Minnesota, and Wisconsin, having been mercilessly exploited and eliminated elsewhere.

Nor did another large predator, *Felis concolor*, escape human persecution. Like the wolf, *Felis concolor* once ranged across the nation, and we have ranged right after it. We have been inconsistent in naming the cats—calling them mountain lions, pumas, cougars, catamounts, or panthers—but we have been thoroughly consistent in our treatment of them: we killed them without remorse. In the East, humans almost entirely eliminated cougars by the turn of the last century. Today, only fifty of the eastern cats are known to survive, all in southern Florida. Isolated and inbred, this population of Florida panthers, as they are commonly known, is on the precipice of extinction. Wildlife managers have resorted to desperate measures to save the subspecies, whose members have several phenotypic signs of a genetic bottleneck, including cowlicks, kinked tails, and cryptochordism (failure of both testicles to descend). Recently, wildlife officials translocated Texas cougars to breed with native Florida panthers as a means of injecting new genetic material into the imperiled population.

People report seeing cougars in other parts of the East with increasing frequency and confidence. These cougars probably were not born in the wild, but were turned loose by exotic pet fanciers who were initially too obtuse to know that cougars are not simply overgrown tabby cats. Yet even if wild cougars do survive, there's little hope that these individuals could spawn stable cougar populations given that the East is so thoroughly inhabited by people. Recolonization is, perhaps, only possible in the large wilderness tracts of northern New England.

In the West, the fever pitch of persecution was also intense over the last 200 years. But the West is vast and highly inaccessible in some areas. Cryptic and highly adaptable, cougars retreated to the most remote mountains and deserts as humans marched west and pursued a scorched earth policy toward large creatures with fangs and claws. It was ecological circumstance, not human design, that saved cougars in the West.

Indeed, humans did their best to stamp out cougars. State and federal policies in the twentieth century reflected cultural contempt for the big cats. States with cougars placed bounties on them, exchanging hard cash for heads and carcasses. Between 1907 and 1978, hunters, ranchers, and damage control agents shot or otherwise killed at least 66,665 cougars in the thirteen western states and provinces. Between 1947 and 1969, the state of Arizona raised the bounty to levels varying between $50 and $100, resulting in a kill of 5,400 lions. California paid out 12,452 cougar bounties between 1907 and 1963, when the legislature terminated the program.

Supplementing the private killing spree, the federal government killed cougars directly through its Animal Damage Control (ADC) program, which Congress reconstituted in 1931. ADC agents, working to eradicate predatory animals "injurious to agriculture," waged a unilateral war against predators with an arsenal of guns, traps, aircraft, and poisons. And while the program served a special interest group—ranchers—it was financed primarily with Americans' tax dollars.

This state-federal cougar pogrom had a thoroughly predictable consequence: it dramatically reduced cougar numbers throughout the West. The Oregon Department of Fish and Wildlife estimated a statewide population of only 200 cougars in 1972, even though the state had millions of acres of suitable cougar habitat on national forests and Bureau of Land Management areas. The same was true for other states in the West—abundant habitat but few inhabitants.

But states softened their cougar policies in the 1960s and early 1970s, ushering in a new era of cougar-human relations. One by one, the states eliminated bounty systems and reclassified cougars as game animals, providing protection for a portion of the year and requiring licensure for private citizens who wished to kill the animals.

The termination of bounty programs served as an indicator of evolving attitudes toward predators. More Americans recognized their value, not only aesthetic but ecological. Some recognized that cougars could have a beneficial impact on deer and elk populations by depressing their irruptions and restoring a cyclical balance between predator and prey.

Eliminating bounties dampened human enthusiasm for killing cougars. Birth rates, probably for the first time in the century, exceeded death rates. With the West having millions of acres of unoccupied or sparsely populated cougar habitat, there were ideal conditions for population growth. And state deer and elk management policies designed to benefit human hunters also proved a boon for nonhuman hunters such as cougars.

As a result, the cougar has steadily reclaimed a substantial portion of its range. The cats now inhabit the rugged—and sometimes not so rugged—lands of Arizona, California, Colorado, Idaho, Montana, Nevada, New Mexico, Oregon, Texas, Utah, Washington, and Wyoming. "It has come back without any costly committees or commissions, without any congressional hearings, without any threatened or endangered status," states Maurice Hornocker, the founder of the Idaho-based Hornocker Wildlife Institute, which fields teams of researchers to study the cats. In Oregon, the Department of Fish and Wildlife estimated the 1996 cougar population at 2,500 lions, while California officials claim that more than 5,000 of the cats survive there. Other state agencies in the West also report sustained population growth, though it's difficult to provide scientifically credible estimates because the animals are so elusive and difficult to count.

With more lions in our midst than perhaps at any other time in this century, we can expect more human-cougar conflicts. The increased cougar population also creates opportunities for trophy hunters, who have exhibited renewed interest in cougar hunting and who are annually amassing a major body count. Ken Logan, one of the nation's leading cougar field biologists, states that trophy hunting is by far the single greatest mortality factor for lions throughout the West.

Trophy hunters kill more than 2,500 lions a year in eleven western states, and many of the hunts are professionally guided. It's not just the trophy hunters' guns and arrows that do damage, but their dogs as well. Some states allow a preseason "pursuit" or "chase" season, when hunters and their dogs can pursue cougars but are forbidden by law from shooting them. These chases not only stress lions and cause them to burn storehouses of energy, but also separate cubs from their mothers. The cubs then may fall prey to bears or cannibalistic adult male cougars. The dogs also take a more direct toll on the cubs. In a study of a hunted cougar population in Utah, Thomas Hemker and his colleagues conclude, "The current sport hunting season in many states begins in the fall, and it is probable that in some areas, cub mortality from maulings and orphaning is as significant as adult harvest."

Even some of the most ruthless hunters can no longer stomach the idea of cougar hunting practices, and there is widespread public opposition to cougar hunting with hounds. Not surprisingly, political campaigns to curtail cougar hunting are fueled by a swirl of emotions. In California, these sentiments boiled over in the late 1980s. The state had protected cougars since 1971, when then-Governor Ronald Reagan imposed a hunting moratorium. The state consistently renewed the moratorium until 1986, when then-Governor George Deukmejian, at the urging of hunters, vetoed a bill to extend it. The state Fish and Game Commission designated hunting zones, fixed license fees, and printed hunting brochures. The revival of hunting was averted only after a series of successful lawsuits in 1987 and 1988 filed by the Mountain Lion Foundation and other animal protection organizations.

Recognizing that the courts would enjoin the hunt for only so long, volunteers began in 1989 the enormous task of gathering signatures to effect a statewide vote on the subject of trophy hunting. Led by activists Bill Yeates, Jerry Meral, and Sharon Negri, thousands of cougar advocates amassed 700,000 signatures and won a place on the June 1990 ballot for Proposition 117, which sought to reclassify the cougar as a "specially protected mammal" and also included major habitat protection provisions. California voters approved the measure and imposed an outright ban on trophy signatures of the cats.

The California initiative spawned similar initiatives in other states. Four years later in Oregon, cougar advocates placed a measure on the ballot to ban hound hunting of cougars and bears and the baiting of bears. Even though trophy hunting groups outspent animal advocates by more than two to one, voters favored an end to hound hunting and baiting. And in Washington, voters in 1996 banned the use of hounds in the hunting of cougars, bears, and bobcats and banned the baiting of bears in a landslide vote.

But a single vote is seldom the last word on a controversial subject. That has already proved true in both California and Oregon. In California, trophy hunting groups challenged the 1990 initiative in the wake of two tragic lion attacks on people. In 1994 a lion killed a jogger in a state recreation area near Auburn, and another lion killed a bird-watcher in a state park near San Diego. Subsequently, the state legislature referred a measure to the March 1996 ballot that would repeal the trophy hunting ban. Trophy hunters argued that cougars were a menace to society: they had already killed two people, and they would kill more. But the public didn't buy the argument. Cougar biologist Rick Hopkins, who had studied the cats in the Diablo Mountains of northern California, placed the risk of a lion attack at one in twenty-five million.

Dr. Paul Beier, who had studied lions in southern California and who had amassed data indicating that there had been about twelve fatal attacks this century and about fifty-five nonfatal attacks throughout all North America, argued not only that the risk of attack was vanishingly small but also that sport hunting would not further diminish the remote possibility of an attack. He cited Vancouver Island, British Columbia, as an example: half of all fatal and nonfatal mountain lion attacks in North America have occurred there, yet its cougar population is one of the most heavily hunted and exploited on the continent. Recent attacks had also occurred in Montana and Colorado, two states permitting cougar hunting.

There's some speculation that trophy hunting may actually increase the likelihood of a lion attack, because trophy hunters tend to take adult males. Beier's research showed that attackers are most often yearlings (both sexes), followed by adult females, with adult males least inclined to attack. When adult males are selectively removed from the population, as in trophy hunting, the proportion of juveniles of either sex in a population increases, boosting the segment of the population most likely to be involved in encounters with people.

Ken Logan, who completed a ten-year cougar study in the San Andres Mountains of New Mexico, wrote to the Oregon legislature when it, too, considered referring a repeal measure to the 1996 ballot. "The increased incidence of lion-human encounters," Logan wrote, "has less to do with the idea that lions are losing their fear of humans than it has to do with our changing management practices and burgeoning human population."

Compared with lion attacks, in fact, threats from other animals and hazards are far more serious. Deer, bees, goats, and even jellyfish account for many more human fatalities than do mountain lions. For every person killed by a lion, 1,200 are struck by lightning and 1,100 are killed in hunting accidents.

In California, on the 1996 revote on the trophy hunting issue, opponents of cougar hunting spent $700,000 delivering their message to voters, while hunting advocates spent $600,000.

When the final attack ads had been aired, voters overwhelmingly rejected lion hunting, defeating the measure by a margin of 16 percent.

In Oregon, the legislature decided not to refer the measure back to the ballot. But hunters took the initiative on their own and gathered 90,000 signatures to place a repeal measure on the November 1996 ballot. The result in Oregon was strikingly similar to that in California. Voters defeated the repeal attempt by 16 percent, affirming the original judgment of voters on the subject. Thus, in six years, there were five statewide votes on the subject of protecting cougars. Each time, voters favored lion protection, handing trophy hunting groups stinging defeats.

State hunting seasons have not been the only target of political activity. So, too, has the federal government's Animal Damage Control program, renamed the Wildlife Services program in 1997. During consideration of the annual congressional appropriations bill that funds the agency, critics of Wildlife Services nearly succeeded in slashing $10 million from its budget—a little less than the total the agency spends on predator control programs in the West.

Yet it would be a mistake to assume that there is an inexorable march toward greater protections for cougars. While the Pacific coast states have favored lion protection through ballot initiatives, and Congress nearly took corrective action, the states in the interior West have ratcheted up lion killing. Responding to the demands of hunting guides and outfitters who want to guide more lion hunts, to hunters who don't like cougars killing deer and elk, and to ranchers fearing their herds could suffer from cougar attacks, the Utah Division of Wildlife has dramatically liberalized its policies regarding lion killing. The kill jumped from 217 cougars in 1990 to 576 cougars in 1997. Kills have increased substantially in Colorado, Idaho, and Montana, among other states.

Utah hunting groups, eyeing the prospect of future initiative attempts by protectionist groups to restrict their sport, have pushed a constitutional amendment onto the state ballot to require a supermajority of two-thirds of voters to establish protections for wildlife. Indeed, the political back-and-forth is not likely to subside. In Oregon, it was not terribly difficult for 1.5 million people to live with 200 cougars in 1972. Now there are 3.2 million people, and perhaps 2,500 cougars. The mix is even more volatile in California, which crowds 32 million people and 5,000 cougars together. It's one matter for voters to disapprove of shooting cougars when it's done in some far-off area. But it's another matter to accept lions in our midst, to take precautions when we hike in the woods, and to know, however fleetingly small the prospect is, that there is a chance we can be attacked by a cougar.

We are engaged in an experiment to determine whether we can live with big, powerful predators. Cougars can and do kill livestock. And they can and do kill people. While the statistical probability of being attacked is extremely remote, statistics seldom comfort people.

The reality is, the conflicts between people and other animals will only become more acute. Expanding in number and in range, people build more homes and businesses in wildlife areas, blaze more roads through habitats, and hike and pursue other recreational activities. We are invading their habitats and crowding them into smaller spaces. It's no surprise that encounters are increasing.

But our feelings toward wildlife are conflicting and confusing. Most people want animals close, but not too close. It's one thing to have a beautiful vista, but it's another to have a beautiful visitor with teeth and claws.

Fundamental questions persist. Is it in our human nature to destroy our competitors? Do we have an impulse to kill and eradicate those species powerful enough and cunning enough to threaten our safety? Do we claim territory and kill off or crowd out competitors?

Human perceptions of the wolf and the grizzly have been radically reconstituted to a significant degree. People don't just value them as commodities or revile them as threats and menaces. Our relationship with them—and with the cougar—is evolving from one based on greed and exploitation to one of compassion and respect. The cougar needs no handouts, no massive recovery plans—just habitat and human tolerance.

Notes on the Contributors

Rick Bass is the author of twelve books of fiction and nonfiction, including *The Sky, the Stars, the Wilderness*, *The Book of Yaak*, *Oil Notes*, *Winter*, *The Watch*, and *The Ninemile Wolves*. He lives with his family in the Yaak Valley in northwestern Montana.

Chris Bolgiano moved to Appalachia in the early 1970s and began writing about ecology and ecotravel. She is the author of *Mountain Lion: An Unnatural History of Pumas and People* and *The Appalachian Forest: A Search for Roots and Renewal*. She has also written for the *New York Times*, *Washington Post*, *Wilderness*, *Audubon*, *Wild Earth*, *American Forests*, and other publications.

Barbara Dean is executive editor of Island Press. She is the author of *Wellspring: A Story from the Deep Country* and has written essays for *Orion*, *Northern Lights*, and other periodicals. She lives and works in northern California.

Jordan Fisher-Smith lives in the Sierra Nevadas, where he has worked as a ranger. His work has appeared in *Orion* and other publications.

Warner Glenn was born in 1936 in Douglas, Arizona, and raised on a cattle ranch at the southern end of the Chiricahua Mountains in southeastern Arizona. He has been a cowboy all his life, and for the last thirty-eight years he has also worked as a big-game hunting guide to help supplement his ranch income. He operates the ranch and hunting business with support from his family and help from his hounds and mules.

Pam Houston's collection of short stories *Cowboys Are My Weakness* was the winner of the 1993 Western States Book Award and has been translated into nine languages. Her second book of fiction, *Waltzing the Cat*, was published in 1998, and a book of essays will appear in 1999. She lives in Colorado at 9,000 feet above sea level, near the headwaters of the Rio Grande.

Verlyn Klinkenborg was born in Colorado and raised in Iowa and California. He has a Ph.D. in English literature from Princeton University and has taught creative writing for many years at Fordham University, Harvard University, and Bennington College. He is the author of *Making Hay* and *The Last Fine Time*, and his work has appeared in numerous magazines. He is now a member of the *New York Times* editorial board.

Ellen Meloy is the author of *The Last Cheater's Waltz* and *Raven's Exile: A Season on the Green River*, winner of a Spur

Award for contemporary nonfiction. The Whiting Foundation honored her with a Writer's Award in 1997. Her natural history essays have been widely anthologized, and she has written for *Orion*, *Northern Lights*, and other journals. She lives on the San Juan River in southern Utah.

M. Cathy Nowak, after more than ten years managing restaurants, returned to school to pursue her dream of working with wildlife. She began at Yakima Valley Community College in Washington state and received her bachelor's degree from Central Washington University. Her experiences with mountain lions came during two years of field research for her master's degree from Washington State University. She currently lives in Oregon.

Wayne Pacelle is senior vice president for communications and government affairs of the Humane Society of the United States in Washington, D.C. He has been instrumental in the passage of legislation protecting predators in several western states.

Diane Josephy Peavey lives on a sheep and cattle ranch in south central Idaho. She writes stories about that life and the changing landscape of the West that are aired weekly on Idaho Public Radio. Her work has appeared in numerous regional publications, including *Boise Magazine*, *The Cabin*, *Range Magazine*, *Imprint*, *Northern Lights*, and the anthology *Where the Morning Light's Still Blue: Personal Essays About Idaho*.

David Quammen is the author of *The Song of the Dodo: Island Biogeography in an Age of Extinctions*, a 1996 *New York Times Book Review* Editor's Choice book. His latest book is *Wild Thoughts from Wild Places*. He is a two-time winner of the National Magazine Award for science essays and other work in *Outside* magazine and is also the recipient of the John Burroughs Medal for natural history writing. He lives in Montana.

Harley G. Shaw worked for the Arizona Game and Fish Department as a research biologist from 1963 until 1990. He spent thirteen years involved in studies of mountain lions, and also studied the Merriam's wild turkey, desert bighorn sheep, and mule deer. In 1989 he hosted the Third Mountain Lion Workshop in Prescott, Arizona. He is the author of *Soul Among Lions: The Cougar as Peaceful Adversary* and *A Mountain Lion Field Guide*. He lives with his wife in Chino Valley, Arizona.

Annick Smith is the author of *Homestead*, the editor of *Headwaters: Montana Writers on Water and Wilderness*, and an editor of *The Last Best Place: A Montana Anthology*. Her work has appeared in a number of publications and anthologies. She has also been a producer of western feature films and documentaries. She lives near the Blackfoot River in Montana.

Jeffery Smith lives with his wife, Lisa Werner, and a houseful of cats in the Appalachian foothills of Coshocton County, Ohio. His first book, *Where the Roots Reach for Water: A Personal Natural History of Melancholia*, will be published in 1999.

E. Donnall Thomas, Jr. writes regularly about bow hunting, wing shooting, fly fishing, and wildlife for a number of national magazines and has written eight books on related subjects, including *Longbow Country* and *Whitefish Can't Jump*. A practicing internist, he lives in rural Montana with his wife Lori, children, Labs, and hounds.

Elizabeth Marshall Thomas has done extensive anthropological fieldwork and is the author of *The Tribe of Tiger*, *The Hidden Life of Dogs*, *Warrior Herdsmen*, *The Harmless People*, *Reindeer Moon*, and *The Animal Wife*. She lives in Peterborough, New Hampshire.

Susan J. Tweit is a field biologist who evolved into a writer and radio commentator. She is the author of six books, including *Seasons in the Desert: A Naturalist's Notebook* and the award-winning children's book *City Foxes*. Her essays and stories have appeared in *Audubon*, *New Mexico*, *Sierra*, *Cricket*, *Bloomsbury Review*, and other magazines. She is also carried by Writers on the Range, an op-ed syndicate run by *High Country News*. She lives in Salida, Colorado, with her husband, Richard Cabe.

Ted Williams has been writing on environmental issues, with special attention to fish and wildlife conservation, since 1970. In addition to freelancing for national magazines, he contributes regular columns to *Audubon* and *Fly Rod & Reel*. In 1997, he was presented with the Conservation Achievement Award by the National Wildlife Federation. He shares an obsession with fishing and bird hunting, but definitely not baseball, with the "real" or, as he prefers, "elder" Ted Williams. He lives with his family in Grafton, Massachusetts.

Terry Tempest Williams is a naturalist and the author of *Pieces of White Shell*, *Coyote's Canyon*, *Refuge: An Unnatural History of Family and Place*, and *Desert Quartet*. The recipient of a Lannan Fellowship in creative nonfiction, she lives in Salt Lake City, Utah, with her husband, Brooke.

Notes on
the Editors

Susan Ewing writes primarily about natural history and the outdoors. She is the author of four books, including *The Great Rocky Mountain Nature Factbook* and *Lucky Hares and Itchy Bears*, an illustrated book of children's verse about northern animals. Her work has also appeared in *Orion*, *Sports Afield*, and *Gray's Sporting Journal*. Susan lives in Montana.

Elizabeth Grossman lives in Portland, Oregon, where she is communications director for Northwest Environment Watch, a nonprofit organization. For more than fifteen years, she worked as a literary agent in New York City. Her work has appeared in *Cascadia Times*, *Orion*, *Sports Afield*, the *New York Times Book Review*, and other publications.

For Further Reading

Bolgiano, Chris, *Mountain Lion: An Unnatural History of Pumas and People* (Stackpole Books, 1995).

Busch, Robert H., *The Cougar Almanac: A Complete Natural History of the Mountain Lion* (Lyons & Burford, 1996).

Davis, Mike, *Ecology of Fear: Los Angeles and the Imagination of Disaster* (Metropolitan Books/Henry Holt & Co., 1998).

Fergus, Charles, *Swamp Screamer: At Large with the Florida Panther* (Farrar, Straus, and Giroux, 1996).

Glenn, Warner, *Eyes of Fire* (Glenn Ranch, P.O. Drawer 1039, Douglas, AZ 85608).

Hansen, Kevin, *Cougar: The American Lion* (Northland Press, 1992).

Nelson, Richard, *Heart and Blood: Living with Deer in America* (Alfred A. Knopf, 1997).

Olson, Dennis L., *Solitary Spirits: Cougars* (NorthWord Press, 1996).

Shaw, Harley G., *Soul Among Lions: The Cougar as Peaceful Adversary* (Johnson Books, 1989).

Thomas, Elizabeth Marshall, *The Tribe of Tiger: Cats and Their Culture* (Simon & Schuster, 1994).

Torres, Steve, *The Mountain Lion Alert: Safety for Outdoor Adventurers and Landowners* (Falcon Press, 1997).

Tweit, Susan J., *Seasons in the Desert: A Naturalist's Notebook*, with illustrations by Kirk Caldwell (Chronicle Books, 1998).

Turner, Jack, *The Abstract Wild* (University of Arizona Press, 1996).

Williams, Terry Tempest, *Coyote's Canyon*, with photographs by John Telford (Peregrine Smith Books, 1989).

Permissions & Sources

"Mountain Lion" by Susan J. Tweit. Copyright © 1998 by Susan J. Tweit. Excerpted from *Seasons in the Desert: A Naturalist's Notebook*. Reprinted by permission of Chronicle Books.

"The Lion's Silent Return" by Ted Williams. Copyright © 1994 by Ted Williams. First published in *Audubon,* November–December, 1994. Reprinted by permission of the author.

"Path of the Puma" by Elizabeth Marshall Thomas. Copyright © 1994 by Elizabeth Marshall Thomas. Excerpted from *The Tribe of Tiger: Cats and Their Culture* (Simon & Schuster). Reprinted by permission of the author.

"Read in Tooth and Claw" by M. Cathy Nowak. Copyright © 1998 by M. Cathy Nowak. Printed by permission of the author.

"On Not Encountering an Eastern Panther" by Chris Bolgiano. Copyright © 1998 by Chris Bolgiano. Printed by permission of the author.

"A Multitude of Witnesses" by Barbara Dean. Copyright © 1997 by Barbara Dean. Appeared in a different version in *Northern Lights,* Fall 1997. Reprinted by permission of the author.

"Lion Eyes" by Terry Tempest Williams. Copyright © 1989 by Terry Tempest Williams. Excerpted from *Coyote's Canyon,* published by Gibbs Smith, Publisher, 1989. Used with permission.

"Looking for Abbey's Lion" by Pam Houston. First appeared in *Whitefish Magazine,* 1998. Reprinted by permission of the author.

"Wildcats I Have Not Known" by Annick Smith. Copyright © 1998 by Annick Smith. Printed by permission of the author.

"Plainchant for the Panther" by Jeffery Smith. Copyright © 1998 by Jeffery Smith. Printed by permission of the author.

"Triangle" by Ellen Meloy. Copyright © 1998 by Ellen Meloy. Printed by permission of the author.

"Riding After Lion" by Verlyn Klinkenborg. Copyright © 1997 by Verlyn Klinkenborg. First published in *Sports Afield*, 1997. Reprinted by permission of the author.

"San Pedro Lion" by Warner Glenn. Copyright © 1998 by Warner Glenn. Printed by permission of the author.

"Lion Story" by Rick Bass. Copyright © 1998 by Rick Bass. Printed by permission of the author.

"A Natural Death" by Jordan Fisher-Smith. Copyright © 1997 by

Index

A

Abbey, Edward, 75–76
Act for Destroying Beasts of Prey
   (South Carolina), 134
Animal Damage Control program,
   201, 206
Appalachia, mountain lions in,
   53–59
Arbuckle, Matthew, 96
Arizona
   bounties, 201
   hunting mountain lions in,
      107–18, 119–26
Armentrout, Dede, 21, 22
Attacks, mountain lion
   on dogs, 35–36, 119–26, 127–32
   fatal, 9, 17, 22–23, 33, 53, 66, 133,
      139–56, 204–05
   on humans, 9, 17, 22–23, 32–38,
      53, 66, 133, 153–54, 204–05
   on livestock, 3, 91, 181–85
Audubon, John James, 91–92
Augustine, Jeff, 13, 15
Autobiography (of Daniel Boone), 91

B

Bear(s)
   grizzly, 199
   and mountain lions, 45
Beier, Paul, 34, 36–38, 204–05
Big Bend Natural Area, 22
Bighorn sheep, and mountain lions,
   21
Bingham family, 183
Bolgiano, Chris, 4

Boone, Daniel, 90
Boulder, mountain lions in, 27–31, 33
Bounties, 16, 93, 135, 150–51, 164,
   201–02
Bow hunting, 159–60
British Columbia
   mountain lions in, 4, 23
   See also Vancouver Island
Bruce, Jay, 97

C

California
   bounties, 201
   legislation, 22, 135–36, 150–51,
      154, 203–04, 205–06
   mountain lions in, 22, 61–70,
      154–55, 207
   See also Los Angeles
Calkins, Franklin Welles, 98
Christianity, animal symbolism in,
   92, 93, 94
Colorado
   legislation, 164
   mountain lions in, 27–33
Cook, John, 119–26
Cougar. *See* mountain lion
Cremony, John C., 91

D

Davis, Mike, 48
Deer, and mountain lions, 10, 17, 18,
   40–42
DeLong, Jim, 97
Denver, mountain lions in, 27, 31
Deukmejian, George, 22, 203

Dogs
　　hunting with, 107–18, 119–26,
　　　152, 169–79, 191, 203
　　attacked by mountain lions,
　　　35–36, 119–26, 127–32

E
Eckhart, Meister, 92
Ecology of Fear, The, 48
Endangered Species Act, 56
Etcheverry family, 183

F
Fifield, Ginny, 187–89, 196
Florida, mountain lions in, 17, 20,
　　56, 58, 200
Folklore, 8, 73
Foster, Jorja, 120–26

G
Game status, mountain lion, 17–18,
　　20, 22 135–36, 151, 164, 203–06
Gamez, Ray, 120–26
Glenn, Marvin, 108, 117
Glenn, Warner, 108–18, 119–26
Glenn, Wendy, 110, 116
Glenn-Kimbro, Kelly, 108–18,
　　119–26
Grizzly bear, population, 199

H
Habitat, mountain lion, 4, 8
　　encroached on by humans, 6, 9,
　　　10–11, 20, 23, 27–38, 61–70,
　　　86, 133–37, 145–48, 151–52,
　　　167, 181–85, 207
Heal, Dan, 22
Hemker, Thomas, 203
Hide, value of, 93
Hopkins, Rick, 204
Hornaday, William T., 48
Hornocker, Maurice, 1–2, 23, 17–20,
　　202
Hornocker Wildlife Institute, 2, 14,
　　19, 202
Huffaker, Steve, 184
Hunting mountain lions, 4, 10, 16,
　　21, 22–23, 34, 107–18, 134–36,
　　150–51, 152, 158–68, 203–07

with a bow, 159–60
with dogs, 107–18, 119–26, 152,
　　169–79, 191, 203
See also bounties; game status

I
Idaho
　　depredation program, 182–83
　　mountain lions in, 181–85
Indians. *See* Native Americans

J
Jaguar(s)
　　in Arizona, 117
　　tracks, 116
Job, Book of, 94, 97, 99
Journey Home, The, 76

K
Kenna, Marie, 153
Kimbro, Kelly Glenn, 108–18,
　　119–26
Kittens, mountain lion, 5–6, 9–10,
　　44–45
Knowles, David, 22–23

L
Leek, S. N., 97
Legislation
　　Act for Destroying Beasts of
　　　Prey (South Carolina), 134
　　California, 22, 135–36, 150–52,
　　　154, 203–04, 205–06
　　Colorado, 164
　　Endangered Species Act, 56
　　Oregon, 204, 206
　　South Carolina, 134
　　Utah, 206–07
　　Washington, 204, 206
　　western United States, 201–02
Leopold, Aldo, 194
Life span, mountain lion, 5–6
Livestock, killed by mountain lions,
　　3, 91, 181–85
Logan, Ken, 13–15, 23–24, 203, 205
Los Angeles, mountain lions in, 48

M

Maine, mountain lions in, 52, 55
Martin, Larry, 21
Maryland, mountain lions in, 55
Mating/reproduction, 5, 9
Mead, Charles, 96
Meral, Jerry, 204
Mills, Enos, 98
Monitoring, 13–25, 187–97
Mountain Lion: An Unnatural History of Pumas and People, 4
Mountain lion(s)
 in Appalachia, 51–59
 in Arizona, 107–18, 119–26
 and bears, 45
 and bighorn sheep, 21
 bounties, 16, 93, 135, 150–51, 164, 201–02
 in British Columbia, 4, 23, 34
 in California, 22, 61–70, 135–36, 154–55, 201, 203–04, 205–06, 207
 call, 96–98
 captive, 57, 101–05
 in Colorado, 27–33, 164
 conservation, 18–19, 22, 151
 cultural significance to Native Americans, 91–93
 and deer, 10, 17, 18, 40–42
 diet, 3, 40
 dogs attacked by, 35–36, 119–26, 127–32
 in eastern United States, 4, 17, 20–21, 51–59, 135, 187–88, 196–97, 200
 edibility of, 158–68
 families, 5, 9–10
 feeding behavior, 43–44, 91
 female, 4–5, 9–10, 44
 in Florida, 17, 20, 56, 58, 200
 folklore, 8, 73
 game status, 17–18, 20, 22 135–36, 151, 164, 203–06
 habitat, 4, 8
 habitat encroached on, 6, 9, 10–11, 20, 23, 27–38, 61–70, 86, 133–37, 145–48, 151–52, 167, 181–85, 207

hide, value of, 93
humans and, 9, 10–11, 16, 20, 22–23, 27–38, 133–37, 133–37
humans attacked by, 9, 17, 22–23, 32–38, 53, 66, 133, 153–54, 204–05
humans killed by, 9, 17, 22–23, 33, 53, 66, 133, 139–56, 204–05
hunting, 4, 10, 16, 21, 22–23, 34, 107–18, 134–36, 150–51, 152, 158–68, 203–07
hunting behavior of, 3, 8–9, 36–38, 40–41, 90–91
hunting with dogs, 107–18, 119–26, 152, 169–79, 191, 203
in Idaho, 181–85
importance of scientific studies of, 13–25, 187–97
kittens, 5–6, 9–10, 44–45
life span, 5–6
livestock killed by, 3, 91, 181–85
in Los Angeles, 48
in Maine, 52, 55
male, 4–5, 9–10, 16, 86
in Maryland, 55
mating/reproduction, 5, 9
monitoring, 13–25, 187–97
names/nicknames for, 2, 7, 13, 47, 99
in Nevada, 4
in New Brunswick, 55, 196
in New Mexico, 21, 23–24
in North Carolina, 89–90
number killed by humans, 10, 23, 31–32, 93, 136, 164, 201, 203, 206
original range, 16, 164, 200
in Paradise Valley, 20
physical characteristics, 2–3, 7–8, 16
population estimates, 3–4, 8, 16–17, 23, 135, 154–55, 201, 202, 207
and prey, 3, 6, 32, 40, 45
radio-tracking, 13–25, 189, 191–93
range, 3–5, 8
religious significance to Native Americans, 94

safety tips, 9, 23, 35–37
sale of as pets, 17, 56–57
in Shenandoah National Park, 56
in South Carolina, 91–92, 134
subspecies, 58–59
in Tennessee, 56
territories, 4–5, 10, 23–24, 58,
    184
in Texas, 17, 21–22, 136
tracking, 187–97
tracks, 3, 72, 81, 116
treatment of kill, 42–44, 121
urban encounters, 6, 8–9, 27–38,
    48, 91, 184
on Vancouver Island, 34, 205
in Vermont, 55
in Virginia, 51–52, 56, 59
in Washington, 136, 204, 206
in western United States, 4,
    135–36, 200–02
and wolves, 45, 177
in Yellowstone National Park, 19
Murphy, Kerry, 20

N

Names and nicknames, 2, 7, 13, 47,
    99
Native Americans
    cultural significance of moun-
        tain lions to, 47–48, 71–74,
        91–93
    religious significance of moun-
        tain lion to, 94
Negri, Sharon, 204
Nevada, mountain lions in, 4
New Brunswick, mountain lions in,
    55, 196
New Mexico, mountain lions in, 21,
    23–24
Noh, Laird, 183
North Carolina, mountain lions in,
    89–90

O

Oregon
    hunting of mountain lions in, 136
    legislation, 204, 206
    mountain lions in, 201, 202, 207

Owen, "Uncle Jim," 97
Oxarango, Roger, 183

P

Panther. See mountain lion
Paradise Valley, mountain lions in,
    20
Perry, W. A., 91
Physical characteristics, 2–3, 7–8, 16
Population estimates, 3–4, 8, 16–17,
    23, 135, 154–55, 201, 202, 207
Prey, mountain lions and, 3, 6, 32,
    40, 45
Proposition 117 (California), 22, 151,
    204
Puma. See mountain lion

R

Radio tracking, 13–25, 189, 191–93
Range, 3–5, 8
    original, 16, 164, 200
    See also territories
Ray, Charles, 14
Reagan, Ronald, 203
Religion, 92, 93, 94
Reproduction. See mating/reproduc-
    tion
Roosevelt, Theodore, 16
Roseland, John "Rosey", 162, 167,
    170, 178

S

Safety tips, 9, 23, 35–37
San Pedro Lion, 119–26
Schoener, Barbara, 22, 133, 139–56
Shaw, Harley, 6, 10
Shenandoah National Park, moun-
    tain lions in, 56
Smith, H. C., 91
Soul Among Lions, 6, 10
Soulen family, 183
South Carolina
    legislation, 134
    mountain lions in, 91–92
Steamboat whistle, mistaken for
    mountain lion's call, 96–97
Stone, Brub, 17–18
Suckley, George, 98
Sweanor, Linda, 15